KEYS TO HIGH-IMPACT CORPORATE GOVERNANCE

BY
ALI KASA

Copyright Notice

© 2025 Ali Kasa. All rights reserved.

No part of this publication may be reproduced, distributed, or transmitted in any form or by any means, including photocopying, recording, or other electronic or mechanical methods, without the prior written permission of the publisher, except in the case of brief quotations embodied in critical reviews and certain other noncommercial uses permitted by copyright law.

DEDICATION

"In the end, we will remember not the words of our enemies, but the silence of our friends."

— Martin Luther King Jr.

I dedicate this book to the brave — the board members, executives, auditors, and GRC professionals who choose to live by their convictions, even when it costs them. This is for those who are willing to endure discomfort, resistance, and personal sacrifice to uphold what they know is right.

To the ones who refuse to look away, who speak when silence would be easier, and who defend integrity when compromise seems more convenient — you embody the moral courage that makes governance not just a framework, but a force for impact.

-Ali Kasa

CONTENTS

PREFACE	**1**
PART I - INTRODUCTION	**3**
Chapter 1: What is Corporate Governance?	5
Chapter 2: What is High-Impact Corporate Governance?	9
Chapter 3: Why High-Impact Governance?	15
PART II - FOUNDATIONS OF IMPACT-DRIVEN GOVERNANCE	**23**
Chapter 4: The Board's New Mandate	25
Chapter 5: Global Baselines of High-Impact Governance	29
Chapter 6: The Governance Standards Landscape	35
Chapter 7: Strategy–Risk Fusion	41
PART III - STRATEGY, RISK & PERFORMANCE	**49**
Chapter 8: Internal Controls for Impact	51
Chapter 9: Governing for Performance	57
Chapter 10: Measuring What Matters	65
Chapter 11: Building Resilience into Strategy	73
PART IV - INTEGRITY, COMPLIANCE & CULTURE	**83**
Chapter 12: The Heart of Governance – Integrity in Action	85
Chapter 13: Compliance as Enabler, Not Burden	91
Chapter 14: Culture – The Invisible Hand of Governance	97
Chapter 15: Ethics, Whistleblowing & Moral Courage	103
PART V - STAKEHOLDERS, SUSTAINABILITY & ESG	**111**
Chapter 16: Stakeholders and the Purpose of the Corporation	113
Chapter 17: ESG as a Governance Imperative	119
Chapter 18: Climate, Environment & Long-Term Governance	125
Chapter 19: Social Responsibility and the Consumer Voice	131
Chapter 20: From ESG to Impact Governance	135

PART VI - TECHNOLOGY, INNOVATION & DIGITAL GOVERNANCE — 143

- Chapter 21: Digital Transformation and the Boardroom — 145
- Chapter 22: Cybersecurity and Digital Resilience — 151
- Chapter 23: Artificial Intelligence, Data Ethics & Governance — 157
- Chapter 24: Innovation, Disruption & the Board's Dilemma — 163

PART VII - GLOBALIZATION, GEOPOLITICS & MULTI-JURISDICTIONAL GOVERNANCE — 171

- Chapter 25: Governing in a Fragmented World — 173
- Chapter 26: Multi-Jurisdictional Governance and Compliance — 179
- Chapter 27: Geopolitics, Sanctions, and Supply Chain Governance — 185
- Chapter 28: Governing Emerging Markets — 191
- Chapter 29: Global Crises and the Role of Governance — 197

PART VIII - AUDIT, ASSURANCE & TRUST — 205

- Chapter 30: The Evolving Role of Audit in Governance — 207
- Chapter 31: Integrated Assurance and the Three Lines Model — 213
- Chapter 32: The Future of Assurance — 219

PART IX - THE FUTURE OF CORPORATE GOVERNANCE — 227

- Chapter 33: The Next Frontier of Governance — 229
- Chapter 34: Technology-Driven Boards of the Future — 235
- Chapter 35 : Global Convergence or Permanent Fragmentation? — 241
- Chapter 36: Governance in 2035 – Scenarios for the Future — 247

PART X - THE KASA HIGH-IMPACT GOVERNANCE SYSTEM TOOLKIT — 255

- Tool 1: The 11 Keys to High-Impact Governance Mindset — 257
- Tool 2: The High-Impact Governance Canvas — 261
- Tool 3: The Strategy–Risk Alignment Matrix — 265
- Tool 4: The Integrated Assurance Map — 267
- Tool 5: The Stakeholder–Impact Heatmap — 269
- Tool 6: The Culture & Integrity Dashboard — 271
- Tool 7: The Performance & Impact Scorecard — 273
- Tool 8: The Board Effectiveness & Maturity Model — 275
- Tool 9: The Crisis & Resilience Readiness Checklist — 277
- Tool 10: The Governance Documentation & Asset Library — 279
- Tool 11: The Authority & Controls Matrix — 281
- Tool 12: The High-Impact Governance Implementation Roadmap — 283

PART XI - THE FUTURE OF GOVERNANCE — 285

    Conclusion — 287
    Epilogue — 291

GLOSSARY — 293

ACRONYMS & ABBREVIATIONS — 297

REFERENCES & FURTHER READING — 299

ACKNOWLEDGMENT OF INFLUENCES — 301

PREFACE

Corporate governance is often spoken of in hushed tones — as if it were a legal necessity, a checklist, or an administrative burden. Too many boardrooms still treat it as a compliance exercise, something to satisfy regulators and investors rather than the lifeblood of long-term value creation. Yet history shows us that governance is not neutral. It either safeguards trust or allows its collapse.

Enron, Wirecard, Petrobras, Luckin Coffee — these names remind us of what happens when governance fails. Fortunes are destroyed, jobs vanish, reputations disintegrate, and public trust evaporates. At the same time, companies like Temasek in Singapore, Tata in India, and Unilever in the UK demonstrate the opposite: governance done right builds resilience, unlocks opportunity, and creates impact that stretches beyond financial returns.

This book, *Keys to High-Impact Corporate Governance*, is written at a Principles of Corporate Governance were updated in 2023 to put sustainability and resilience at the heart of board duties. The UK Corporate Governance Code 2024 tightens accountability for internal controls. The International Sustainability Standards Board has set a global baseline for climate and sustainability disclosures. Cybersecurity, AI ethics, data privacy, and stakeholder capitalism have all become board-level imperatives.

In this shifting landscape, boards, CEOs, chief strategy officers, risk professionals, auditors, and governance leaders face a stark choice: adapt and lead, or lag and risk irrelevance. This book is written to help them lead.

PREFACE

Unlike many governance texts that remain abstract or confined to Western contexts, this work aims to be globally balanced and practically applied. You will find lessons from Asia, the Middle East, Africa, and emerging markets alongside Europe and North America. You will encounter both success stories and cautionary tales. Each chapter will open with a case, unpack the latest global standards, highlight the key takeaways, and conclude with practical tools for application in your own boardroom.

This book is not a checklist. It is a call to courage. Governance is not about avoiding failure; it is about enabling impact. It is about board members who are willing to ask hard questions, executives who align risk with strategy, auditors who provide assurance with integrity, and professionals across the governance, risk, and compliance (GRC) spectrum who insist that doing the right thing is not optional — it is existential.

If you are holding this book, you are likely one of them. You are someone who believes that governance is not paperwork but purpose; not bureaucracy but bravery; not theory but the practice of moral courage.

May these pages equip you, challenge you, and above all, embolden you to govern for impact.

PART I
INTRODUCTION

CHAPTER 1
What is Corporate Governance?

"Good corporate governance is about 'intellectual honesty' and not just sticking to rules and regulations. Capitalism's trustworthiness is at stake."

— MERVYN KING, CHAIR OF THE KING COMMISSION ON GOVERNANCE IN SOUTH AFRICA

In the late 1990s, Enron Corporation proudly published its corporate values: **Communication. Respect. Integrity. Excellence.** On paper, it looked flawless. The company projected itself as a model of modern business, guided by strong principles and innovative governance. But in reality, these values were betrayed daily. Enron's executives created a culture of deception, hiding massive debts and inflating profits.

When the truth emerged in 2001, Enron collapsed almost overnight. More than 20,000 employees lost their jobs, shareholders lost $74 billion, and pensions vanished. It became one of the largest bankruptcies in history — a cautionary tale that governance cannot be cosmetic. It must be lived.

Governance Beyond Paper
Enron's story illustrates a fundamental truth about governance: when it exists only in words, it fails. Structures, committees, and codes cannot protect a company if leaders lack accountability and moral courage.

Yet, at its heart, **corporate governance is neither a formality nor a burden. It is the system by which an organization is directed, controlled, and held accountable. It is the architecture of trust.** Governance determines who makes decisions, how they are made, and for whose benefit. It is about power, accountability, and responsibility.

From Steering Ships to Steering Companies

The very word governance comes from the Latin *gubernare*, meaning *to steer*. Ancient navigators relied on governance to guide their vessels across stormy seas. Today, companies face their own storms — market volatility, technological disruption, societal expectations, and climate risk. Governance is the compass and the rudder that keep the organization on course.

The Rise of Modern Governance

Modern corporate governance grew out of crisis. The Cadbury Report (1992) in the UK introduced principles of accountability, independence, and transparency. In the US, the Sarbanes-Oxley Act (2002) followed directly from the implosions of Enron and WorldCom. Globally, frameworks evolved — South Africa's King Reports (culminating in King IV), Japan's Corporate Governance Code (2015, revised 2021), and the ASEAN Corporate Governance Scorecard. The OECD Principles of Corporate Governance, revised most recently in 2023, serve as a benchmark worldwide.

Despite these advances, many organizations still treat governance as compliance — a binder of rules to display, not a living system to guide decisions.

Why Governance Matters

Enron had all the appearances of good governance — committees, codes, and values. But appearances are not enough. Governance matters only when boards and executives practice it with integrity, curiosity, and courage.

The lesson is simple: **corporate governance is not about what is written; it is about what is lived.**

Takeaways & Reflections

The collapse of Enron reminds us that governance cannot be measured by the presence of policies, committees, or glossy value statements. It is measured by how leaders act when faced with pressure, complexity, or temptation. True governance lives in practice, not on paper. It is the architecture of trust that directs, controls, and holds leaders accountable for their decisions.

As you close this chapter, pause and reflect on how these lessons apply to your own organization:

Reflection 1: Values in Action

Enron had the right values written down — Communication, Respect, Integrity, Excellence — but they were ignored in practice. What values has your organization declared, and how visible are they in daily decisions and behaviors?

_____

_____

_____

Reflection 2: Governance as Trust

Does governance in your organization build genuine trust among investors, employees, and society, or is it seen mainly as a compliance burden?

_____

_____

_____

Reflection 3: From Paper to Practice

Think of your board charter, policies, or committee structures. Are they guiding real choices, or do they exist mainly for regulators and auditors? How can you make them more alive?

_____

_____

_____

CHAPTER 2
What is High-Impact Corporate Governance?

> *"Good governance never depends upon laws, but upon the personal qualities of those who govern. The machinery of government is always subordinate to the will of those who administer that machinery."*
>
> — FRANK HERBERT

Most organizations today can point to governance structures: a board charter, an audit committee, compliance policies, and an ethics code. They may even publish governance reports filled with carefully worded assurances. Yet, in practice, many of these systems exist only in form, not in function. Governance becomes performance — a show for regulators, auditors, or investors — rather than a living framework that guides decisions and protects trust.

High-impact corporate governance is different. It refuses to stop at formality. It insists that governance should **shape real behavior, real choices, and real outcomes**. It is not satisfied with a company that looks good on paper but fails its people, its shareholders, or society. High-impact governance seeks to answer a deeper question: *What difference does our governance make?*

Case Study: Tata Group – Governance That Withstood a Storm

In 2016, the Tata Group of India — a conglomerate spanning steel, cars, IT, hotels, and more — faced a storm that could have shattered its reputation. The group's chairman, Cyrus Mistry, was abruptly removed in a dramatic boardroom battle. Accusations flew between the Tata Trusts, which controlled the group, and Mistry's camp. The crisis spilled into the public domain, and the once unshakeable image of Tata as a beacon of integrity seemed at risk.

Yet the group did not collapse. Instead, Tata emerged from the crisis with renewed strength. Its governance structures were stress-tested but not destroyed. Reforms followed: clearer roles for the Tata Trusts, greater transparency in succession planning, and stronger emphasis on independent oversight. The group weathered the storm and rebuilt confidence.

Tata's story shows us that high-impact governance does not mean the absence of conflict. Rather, it means having systems and values strong enough to recover from crisis and emerge stronger. Where governance is merely cosmetic, crises destroy. Where governance is high-impact, crises refine.

The Principles of High-Impact Governance

What, then, distinguishes high-impact governance? The answer lies not in more committees or longer codes, but in principles that animate the way organizations are led.

High-impact governance begins with **clarity of purpose**. A company exists for more than profit; it exists to create value for society, for employees, and for future generations. Governance ensures that purpose is not an inspiring statement on a website, but the North Star guiding boardroom decisions.

It demands **accountability with integrity**. Structures matter — independent directors, transparent reporting, effective committees — but these only have value when matched by the courage to act, to question, and to challenge management when necessary. Integrity is not built into documents; it is carried by people.

It aligns **strategy with risk appetite**. Every company faces risk, but only those with high-impact governance integrate risk management into strategic decision-making. Boards that understand their appetite for risk — and how much they are willing to stake for growth — can balance ambition with resilience.

It requires **transparency and stewardship**. High-impact governance is stewardship: the recognition that leaders do not own the company but hold it in trust for shareholders, stakeholders, and society. Transparency is the currency of trust, and stewardship is the responsibility to protect long-term value, even at the cost of short-term convenience.

It insists on **sustainability and resilience**. Governance that focuses only on quarterly results is fragile. High-impact governance equips boards to consider the impact of today's decisions on the environment, on communities, and on the company's ability to endure shocks tomorrow.

And finally, it is anchored in **culture and moral courage**. No policy can substitute for the courage of a leader who chooses to do the right thing when the easier option is to remain silent. High-impact governance lives in the culture of an organization — in whether employees feel safe to speak up, in whether decisions reflect values, and in whether leaders model the behavior they demand of others.

Key Takeaways

The lesson is clear: governance that is limited to structures and codes will always remain fragile. High-impact governance breathes life into those structures by embedding purpose, accountability, stewardship, sustainability, and culture into the daily reality of decisions. Organizations that embrace these principles may still face crises, but they will have the resilience to recover. Those that ignore them may look solid on the surface, but they are hollow within.

How to Apply and Reflect

As you consider these principles, pause and reflect on your own context. Use the lines below to capture your thoughts — not as a test, but as a mirror.

Reflection 1: Purpose

What is the true purpose of my organization, beyond profit, and how does our governance ensure that purpose drives decisions?

_____

_____

_____

Reflection 2: Accountability and Integrity

When was the last time our board demonstrated moral courage by challenging management or resisting pressure to compromise?

_____

_____

_____

Reflection 3: Risk and Strategy

Do we have a clear statement of our risk appetite, and do we test strategic decisions against it?

_____

_____

_____

Reflection 4: Stewardship and Transparency

In what ways are we acting as stewards of long-term value rather than managers of short-term performance?

_____

_____

_____

Reflection 5: Sustainability and Culture

How visible is our commitment to sustainability and ethical culture in the daily life of the organization?

_____

_____

_____

High-impact governance is not about adding more documents to a binder. It is about creating alignment between purpose, risk, culture, and outcomes. And it begins with the willingness of leaders to ask difficult questions — and to write honest answers

CHAPTER 3
Why High-Impact Governance?

"Corporate governance is not just about structures and processes. It is about values, integrity, and the courage to do what is right — especially when it is difficult."

— Adapted from Mervyn King

The question is not whether corporate governance is necessary. The evidence is overwhelming: companies that lack governance collapse under the weight of mismanagement, fraud, or loss of trust. The real question is *why* governance matters, and why the era of **high-impact corporate governance** has arrived.

Too often, companies treat governance as a legal necessity or a public relations exercise. Boards adopt policies and committees to show compliance, but these rarely influence how decisions are made. This mindset explains why scandals repeat across industries and geographies: because governance is reduced to appearances.

The truth is stark: **corporate governance is not optional. It is the difference between companies that endure and those that vanish.**

A Brief History of Governance: Born from Scandal, Shaped by Crisis

The modern story of corporate governance is one of crisis and reform. Each generation of failures produced new frameworks designed to restore trust.

In the early 1990s, the collapse of Maxwell Communications and the BCCI banking scandal led to the **Cadbury Report (1992)** in the UK, which first set out principles of accountability, board independence, and audit oversight. A decade later, Enron and WorldCom imploded in the United States, wiping out billions in shareholder value and shaking global confidence. In response, Congress enacted the **Sarbanes-Oxley Act (2002)**, imposing strict internal control and financial reporting requirements.

Around the world, similar reforms followed: South Africa pioneered the **King Reports**, Japan introduced its **Corporate Governance Code** (2015, revised 2021), ASEAN launched a **Corporate Governance Scorecard** to raise standards across the region, and Saudi Arabia's **Capital Market Authority** established regulations to professionalize boards and increase transparency. The **OECD Principles of Corporate Governance**, first published in 1999 and most recently updated in 2023, remain the global benchmark.

History shows that governance advances only after painful failures. The challenge for today's leaders is whether they can build **impact-driven governance** without waiting for the next disaster to force their hand.

Case Study: Luckin Coffee – Growth Without Governance

In 2017, Luckin Coffee burst onto the scene in China as a challenger to Starbucks. With aggressive expansion and slick marketing, it grew at lightning speed, opening thousands of stores in just two years. Investors poured in billions, and in 2019 Luckin was listed on NASDAQ.

Behind the scenes, however, governance was weak. Internal controls were inadequate, oversight was superficial, and the pressure to deliver growth at any cost created a culture of corner-cutting. By 2020, it was revealed that executives had fabricated over $300 million in sales. The scandal sent shockwaves across global markets. Luckin's shares were delisted, its reputation destroyed, and investors lost billions.

The lesson is clear: rapid growth without governance is unsustainable. Luckin had the appearance of success, but no foundation of trust. It demonstrated that governance is not a luxury for mature companies — it is a prerequisite for survival, no matter how fast a business is growing.

Why Corporate Governance Matters

Governance matters because it protects the most fragile asset any company has: trust. Investors trust that their capital is being used wisely. Employees trust that leadership will treat them fairly. Customers trust that promises will be kept. Society trusts that companies will not enrich themselves at the expense of the common good. When governance fails, that trust evaporates — and with it, the company's license to operate.

Governance also matters because it connects power with responsibility. Modern corporations wield enormous influence, sometimes greater than states. Without governance, that power can be abused. With governance, it can be directed toward innovation, growth, and value creation.

Why High-Impact Governance Matters Now

If governance has always been necessary, why speak of *high-impact governance* today? The answer lies in the changing environment. The 21st century has introduced risks and responsibilities that traditional governance frameworks alone cannot address.

Climate change demands that boards consider sustainability and resilience, not just profit. Cybersecurity and artificial intelligence create new ethical dilemmas and existential risks. Stakeholders, from employees to consumers, expect more transparency and responsibility. Regulators are tightening standards, investors are demanding ESG disclosures, and society is holding companies accountable as never before.

High-impact governance is the only response adequate to this new reality. It ensures that governance is not just about survival, but about leadership — about boards that steer their companies to create long-term value for shareholders and society alike.

Key Takeaways

The history of governance proves one thing: weak governance destroys value, while strong governance builds resilience. The scandals of the past remind us that compliance is never enough. Today's challenges — from climate to cyber — demand governance that is active, courageous, and purposeful. High-impact governance is no longer optional; it is the new baseline for enduring success.

How to Apply and Reflect

Reflection 1: Learning from History

What past governance failure (Enron, WorldCom, Luckin, or others) resonates most with my organization, and what lessons should we internalize before we repeat them?

Reflection 2: Governance as Trust

In what ways is trust at risk in my organization today — among investors, employees, customers, or society — and how can governance strengthen it?

_____

_____

_____

Reflection 3: Rising to New Challenges

How prepared is my board to govern emerging risks such as sustainability, cybersecurity, or artificial intelligence? What practical steps should we take this year?

_____

_____

_____

Corporate governance matters because companies exist within a web of trust and accountability. High-impact governance matters because the challenges of our age demand more than compliance. They demand courage, foresight, and the willingness to steer not only for today, but for generations to come.

Part I Summary – Understanding Corporate Governance

Corporate governance has often been misunderstood, reduced to binders of policies and compliance checklists. Yet as we saw in Part I, governance is far more than paperwork. It is the **architecture of trust** — the system by which an organization is directed, controlled, and held accountable.

We began with Enron, a company whose values of *Communication, Respect, Integrity, and Excellence* looked flawless on paper but were betrayed in practice. Its collapse revealed the truth that governance is measured not by structures but by courage and execution.

We then explored **High-Impact Governance**, which goes beyond compliance to outcomes. Through Tata's resilience and reform, we saw that high-impact governance lives in purpose, accountability, risk alignment, transparency, sustainability, and culture. It is governance that makes a difference.

Finally, we asked why governance — and especially high-impact governance — matters now. The history of codes and scandals shows that governance evolves through crisis. From Cadbury to Sarbanes-Oxley, from King IV to OECD 2023, the lesson is constant: weak governance destroys value, while strong governance builds resilience. Today, with risks such as climate, cyber, and AI, the stakes are higher than ever. Governance must not only protect companies but enable them to lead responsibly.

Reflection Pause

How alive are our governance values in daily practice?

Do we treat governance as compliance or as impact?

What lessons from past failures (Enron, Luckin, others) apply most urgently to us today?

Part I left us with a clear mandate: governance is not a formality but a force. High-impact governance is the only credible path forward.

PART II
FOUNDATIONS OF IMPACT-DRIVEN GOVERNANCE

CHAPTER 4
The Board's New Mandate

"Boards of directors are not there to run companies. They are there to ensure companies are run well — in the interests of shareholders, stakeholders, and society at large."

— Sir Adrian Cadbury

For decades, the role of boards was defined narrowly: safeguard shareholder value, appoint the CEO, and sign off on major decisions. Governance codes were written with this limited purpose in mind. But the world has changed. Stakeholders now expect boards to go beyond compliance and oversight. They demand leadership that considers long-term impact, not just quarterly results.

This is the new mandate of boards: to act as **stewards of purpose and trust**, not merely guardians of financial statements. Boards must define where a company is going, why it exists, and how it creates value for all stakeholders.

Case Study: Singapore Airlines – Purpose as Strategy

Singapore Airlines (SIA) is consistently ranked among the best airlines in the world. Its governance provides a striking example of how a board can align purpose with strategy to sustain excellence over decades.

From the start, SIA's board and leadership defined its purpose not simply as "air travel," but as **delivering exceptional service and safety with a**

uniquely Singaporean standard of quality. This purpose guided investment decisions, culture, and risk management. Even in crises — from SARS in 2003 to COVID-19 in 2020 — the board anchored decisions in this purpose. It approved large investments in fleet renewal and service training even when profitability was under pressure, because it recognized that purpose-driven strategy builds resilience.

The outcome speaks for itself: SIA emerged from the pandemic with record profits in 2023 and a reputation not only intact but enhanced. Its governance model demonstrates that when boards embrace purpose as their mandate, they create organizations capable of weathering storms and seizing opportunities.

Contrast this with **Wirecard**, once celebrated as a rising star in European fintech. Its board failed to question management's too-good-to-be-true growth, ignored whistleblowers, and allowed governance to serve appearances instead of truth. Wirecard collapsed in 2020 under the weight of a €1.9 billion fraud, becoming Germany's biggest postwar accounting scandal.

Two companies. Two boards. One treated purpose as its compass, the other treated compliance as its shield. One thrived; the other imploded.

The Board's New Mandate Explained

High-impact governance reframes the role of boards in three critical ways:

First, boards must lead with purpose. Purpose is not a marketing slogan. It is the reason the company exists, and boards are the custodians of this reason. The **OECD Principles (2023, Chapter II.A)** emphasize that boards are responsible for setting the company's strategic direction and ensuring that long-term objectives are consistent with its purpose and values. Without this anchor, boards drift, and companies chase growth at any cost.

Second, boards must embrace stakeholder accountability. Shareholders matter, but so do employees, customers, suppliers, regulators, and society. The **OECD Principles (2023, Chapter I.A)** recognize that boards must take into account the interests of stakeholders, particularly in areas like sustainability, resilience, and risk management, because these directly affect long-term shareholder value. A board that ignores stakeholders undermines its own company's survival.

Third, boards must cultivate culture and moral courage. Tone from the top is more than words in an annual report. It is visible in how directors question management, how they respond to whistleblowers, and how they handle crises. The **OECD Principles (2023, Chapter V.A)** highlight the board's responsibility to oversee disclosure and transparency — but disclosure without culture is hollow. High-impact boards make culture a priority, ensuring integrity is practiced at every level of the organization.

Takeaways & Reflections

The new mandate of boards is not to do more paperwork or create more committees. It is to lead with purpose, to hold themselves accountable to stakeholders, and to build cultures of integrity and courage. These are not abstract ideals; they are practical necessities for companies navigating today's risks.

As you reflect on this chapter, consider these questions for your own context:

Reflection 1: Purpose at the Center

How clearly is our organization's purpose defined, and in what ways does the board ensure that purpose guides strategy and decisions?

_____

_____

_____

Reflection 2: Stakeholder Accountability

Beyond shareholders, who are the stakeholders most affected by our board's decisions, and how do we make their interests visible in our governance discussions?

_____

_____

_____

Reflection 3: Culture and Courage

What examples can I point to where our board demonstrated moral courage — asking the uncomfortable question, resisting the easy compromise, or setting the tone for integrity?

_____

_____

_____

A board that treats governance as compliance will always be reactive, waiting for the next crisis to dictate reforms. A board that embraces its new mandate — to steward purpose, accountability, and culture — becomes proactive, resilient, and trusted. This is the essence of high-impact corporate governance.

CHAPTER 5
Global Baselines of High-Impact Governance

"Good governance is a journey, not a destination. It evolves as society's expectations evolve, and it fails when companies forget that legitimacy is earned, not assumed."

— Adapted from King IV

Corporate governance has never been a one-size-fits-all concept. Across the world, different markets have built their own codes, shaped by culture, history, and legal traditions. Yet today, a striking convergence is taking place. Whether in London or Johannesburg, Singapore or Riyadh, boards are being asked to step beyond compliance into stewardship. This convergence is creating a **global baseline for high-impact governance**.

Case Study: Unilever – From UK Code to Global Consumer Trust

Unilever, the Anglo-Dutch multinational, has long been governed under the UK Corporate Governance Code. The Code demands board independence, accountability for internal controls, and fair treatment of shareholders. But Unilever went further. Guided by its purpose — "to make sustainable living commonplace" — its governance integrated stakeholder voices into strategy.

When the UK Code was revised in 2024, it tightened requirements on internal control effectiveness (Provision 29). Unilever was already ahead of the curve. Its board linked internal controls not only to financial risk but to environmental and social impact reporting. This forward-looking approach has helped the company maintain resilience in volatile markets, but also built consumer trust. At a time when boycotts and public backlash can collapse reputations overnight, Unilever demonstrates that governance aligned with purpose and stakeholders is not charity — it is survival.

The Convergence of Governance Codes

The **OECD Principles of Corporate Governance (2023)** now explicitly require boards to consider sustainability and resilience in strategy. Chapter II emphasizes the role of boards in setting purpose and long-term objectives, while Chapter I recognizes the importance of stakeholders in sustaining long-term value.

The **UK Corporate Governance Code (2024)** sharpened expectations for internal control effectiveness, requiring boards to attest to and explain how their systems work in practice — a move away from box-ticking toward accountability.

King IV (South Africa) stands out for its "apply and explain" philosophy, making governance outcomes-based rather than compliance-driven. It emphasizes integrated thinking, ethical leadership, and combined assurance — themes that resonate with high-impact governance.

The **ASEAN Corporate Governance Scorecard** pushes boards in Southeast Asia toward higher disclosure standards and board professionalism, raising the bar in emerging markets.

Meanwhile, **international standards** such as **ISO 37000 (governance), ISO 37301 (compliance),** and **ISO 37001 (anti-bribery)** provide practical frameworks that can be applied across geographies, while the **ISSB's IFRS S1/S2** has created the first global baseline for sustainability and climate disclosures.

Together, these frameworks are forming a tapestry: not identical, but increasingly harmonized around the same principles — purpose, accountability, sustainability, resilience, and transparency.

The Future of Corporate Governance: The Consumer Voice

Historically, governance was about two groups: shareholders and management. But today, **consumers are entering the governance equation** in ways boards cannot ignore.

In 2023–2024, global boycotts erupted against companies perceived to support wars, human rights violations, or unethical government policies. For example, companies linked — directly or indirectly — to the war on Gaza faced consumer backlash and organized boycotts. PepsiCo faced reputational challenges when it was criticized for its perceived alignment with U.S. immigration policies and treatment of foreign workers. In both cases, governance structures were tested not by regulators, but by ordinary people with smartphones, hashtags, and wallets.

Consumers are voting with their money, and their voices now shape corporate legitimacy as much as regulators or investors. High-impact governance must therefore expand accountability: not just to investors and regulators, but to the communities and consumers that grant companies their license to operate.

This is the future of governance — **a multi-stakeholder compact** where boards must weigh not only compliance and profit but also legitimacy in the eyes of society.

Takeaways & Reflections

The global baseline of governance is converging around the same themes: purpose, accountability, sustainability, and transparency. But the real shift is in who holds companies accountable. Regulators enforce codes, investors demand returns, but consumers now wield a veto over legitimacy.

As you close this chapter, consider these questions for your own context:

Reflection 1: Global Alignment

Which global governance codes or standards (OECD, UK, King IV, ASEAN, ISSB, ISO) do we currently benchmark against, and where are our gaps?

Reflection 2: Internal Controls with Impact

If our board had to attest — today — to the effectiveness of our internal controls, would we be able to show not only compliance, but impact on sustainability and resilience?

Reflection 3: The Consumer Voice

How visible are consumers in our governance discussions? Have we assessed how our positions on social issues, government policy, or human rights could trigger boycotts or reputational risk?

_____

_____

_____

_____

The future of governance will not be decided in regulators' offices alone. It will be shaped in boardrooms, but also in supermarkets, on social media, and in the collective conscience of society. Companies that embrace this broader accountability will thrive. Those who resist it will discover that governance failures are punished not just by markets, but by people.

CHAPTER 6
The Governance Standards Landscape

"Codes of governance are like lighthouses: they do not steer the ship, but they warn of dangers and mark the way forward."

— ALI KASA

Corporate governance is not a single code or standard. It is a mosaic of frameworks developed over decades, across markets, and often born from crisis. For new directors, executives, or professionals, the sheer number of standards can feel overwhelming. Yet knowing the landscape is essential. Standards and codes are the **benchmarks of trust** — they define what good governance looks like, and they provide boards with a compass for accountability. This chapter surveys the most influential frameworks, from the first modern codes to today's international standards and regional practices, and asks: *which ones should your board use as reference?*

The Early Codes

The modern governance movement began with the **Cadbury Report (UK, 1992)**, which introduced principles of board independence, separation of chairman and CEO, and audit committee oversight. Cadbury marked the start of governance as a discipline in its own right, not just an extension of company law. In 1999, the **OECD Principles of Corporate Governance** were published, creating the first globally recognized benchmark. Revised most recently in 2023, they emphasize sustainability,

THE GOVERNANCE STANDARDS LANDSCAPE

resilience, and stakeholder accountability as board responsibilities. In the United States, the collapse of Enron and WorldCom led to the **Sarbanes-Oxley Act (SOX, 2002)**, which revolutionized internal control and financial reporting. Meanwhile, South Africa's **King Reports** (starting in 1994, culminating in King IV in 2016) pioneered "integrated thinking" and "apply and explain" governance, making outcomes more important than compliance. Together, these codes laid the foundations for high-impact governance.

International Standards

As governance matured, international standards emerged to provide universal benchmarks. **ISO 37000 (2021)** set out principles for the governance of organizations, applicable across industries and jurisdictions. **ISO 37301** established a global standard for compliance management systems, while **ISO 37001** (anti-bribery) addressed one of governance's most persistent risks. Beyond ISO, the **COSO Frameworks** — Internal Control (2013) and Enterprise Risk Management (2017) — became the lingua franca of boards and auditors worldwide. The **International Sustainability Standards Board (ISSB)** introduced IFRS S1 and S2 in 2023, setting a global baseline for sustainability and climate disclosures. And the **Institute of Internal Auditors (IIA)** updated its **Global Internal Audit Standards (2024)** and **Three Lines Model**, making clear how assurance should function across organizations. These standards equip boards with the language and tools to translate governance into practice.

Key Markets

Different regions have tailored governance to their contexts, yet all are converging on similar principles. In the **United States**, SOX remains central, alongside NYSE and Nasdaq listing rules, which require independent directors, audit committees, and governance disclosures. The **United**

Kingdom Corporate Governance Code (2024) emphasizes board accountability for internal control effectiveness and long-term stewardship. In the **European Union**, directives such as the Shareholder Rights Directive II and the Corporate Sustainability Reporting Directive (CSRD) embed shareholder engagement and ESG disclosures into governance obligations. Across **Asia**, Japan's Corporate Governance Code (2015, revised 2021) stresses transparency in cross-shareholdings, while India's SEBI regulations demand strong audit and risk committees. The **ASEAN Corporate Governance Scorecard** benchmarks companies across Southeast Asia, raising standards in emerging markets. In the **GCC**, Saudi Arabia's Capital Market Authority (CMA) has established rigorous governance regulations, while the UAE and Qatar have introduced their own governance codes, often aligning with OECD and IFRS guidance. Each of these market-specific frameworks reflects local realities while reinforcing global norms.

Which Code to Use as Reference?

Boards often ask: which standard should we follow? The answer depends on context. Multinational companies should benchmark against **OECD Principles** and **ISO 37000**, ensuring they align with the global baseline. Listed companies must comply with their **local securities regulator's code**, whether that is SOX in the US, the UK Code, or Saudi CMA regulations. Family businesses and SMEs, though not always bound by law, benefit from **King IV**, with its focus on outcomes, ethics, and integrated thinking. Risk and compliance professionals should look to **COSO, ISO 37301, and the IIA Standards**, which provide practical guidance for implementing governance at the operational level. The best boards are not content with meeting the minimum — they benchmark locally but aspire to international best practice.

The Future of Standards

Governance is still evolving. The future will see greater harmonization between frameworks, with the **OECD Principles** and **ISSB sustainability standards** becoming global anchors. ESG will move from voluntary disclosure to mandatory accountability. **AI governance** is emerging, with **ISO/IEC 42001** and the **NIST AI Risk Management Framework** setting early benchmarks. The focus will shift from "comply or explain" to "apply and evidence," where boards must show not only that governance structures exist, but that they are effective in shaping decisions and culture. In this future, codes and standards will matter less as binders and more as proof — evidence that governance creates real-world impact.

Takeaways & Reflections

The governance landscape is rich, complex, and still growing. For new directors and professionals, the challenge is not to memorize every standard but to know which ones apply — and how to use them as references for building high-impact governance.

Reflection 1: The Map of Standards

Which of these standards or codes guide my board today, and are they enough to meet the expectations of investors, regulators, and society?

_____

_____

_____

_____

Reflection 2: Benchmarking Ambition

If my organization benchmarked against ISO 37000, OECD 2023, or King IV, what gaps would appear, and what would it take to close them?

_____

_____

_____

_____

_____

Reflection 3: Preparing for the Future

Are we preparing for the next wave of governance standards — ESG disclosures, AI oversight, consumer-driven accountability — or are we still focused only on yesterday's requirements?

_____

_____

_____

_____

_____

By understanding the governance standards landscape, boards equip themselves with a compass. No code or standard guarantees success, but knowing which lighthouses to follow can mean the difference between drifting aimlessly and steering with confidence toward impact

CHAPTER 7
Strategy–Risk Fusion

"Risk is not a separate conversation from strategy. Strategy without risk is blind, and risk without strategy is meaningless."

— ALI KASA

Defining Strategy and Risk

Every company speaks about strategy, yet few define it with precision. Strategy is not a collection of projects or annual budgets. At its core, **strategy is the deliberate set of choices a company makes to create value and sustain competitive advantage over time**. It answers three fundamental questions: *Where will we compete? How will we win? What capabilities must we build to sustain that advantage?*

Risk, on the other hand, is often misunderstood as merely negative events. In reality, **risk is the effect of uncertainty on objectives** (ISO 31000). It includes threats that could prevent success but also opportunities that, if seized, could accelerate value creation. In governance terms, risk is not about eliminating uncertainty — it is about steering through it.

When boards discuss strategy without risk, they are charting a course without considering storms. When they discuss risk without strategy, they are counting waves without knowing the destination. High-impact governance fuses the two.

COSO ERM and the Fusion Framework

The **Committee of Sponsoring Organizations of the Treadway Commission (COSO)** developed the **Enterprise Risk Management (ERM) Framework**, updated in 2017, which remains the global benchmark for aligning risk with strategy. COSO ERM emphasizes that risk management is not an isolated function; it must be embedded in **strategy-setting and performance management**.

At its heart, COSO ERM integrates:

- **Governance and culture** → the foundation for oversight and risk awareness.
- **Strategy and objective-setting** → defining risk appetite in relation to business goals.
- **Performance** → identifying and assessing risks that could impact objectives.
- **Review and revision** → ensuring resilience as environments change.
- **Information, communication, and reporting** → delivering insights to decision-makers.

Boards that apply COSO ERM move beyond defensive thinking. They use risk to sharpen choices, balance ambition with resilience, and ensure accountability for both upside and downside outcomes.

The Role of Risk Appetite

Central to strategy–risk fusion is the concept of **risk appetite**: the amount and type of risk an organization is willing to accept in pursuit of its objectives. Risk appetite is not a fixed number — it is a set of boundaries that guide decision-making.

For example, a growth strategy in emerging markets may be attractive, but only if the board is comfortable with higher political and regulatory risk. Investing in artificial intelligence may be strategic, but only if the organization is prepared to manage ethical, reputational, and cybersecurity risks.

The **OECD Principles (2023, Chapter II)** explicitly state that boards should oversee risk management and ensure that risk appetite is aligned with long-term objectives. Without this alignment, strategy becomes reckless ambition, and risk management becomes bureaucratic caution. Together, they form a compass.

Case Study: Archegos Capital – When Risk and Strategy Were Misaligned

In 2021, Archegos Capital Management, a private investment firm, collapsed almost overnight, triggering over $10 billion in losses for global banks. Archegos's strategy relied on concentrated bets in a handful of stocks, financed through highly leveraged derivatives called total return swaps.

The risk was clear: excessive leverage combined with lack of transparency. Yet banks extended credit lines without fully understanding Archegos's strategy or assessing whether the risk exposure aligned with their own appetites. When stock prices fell, Archegos defaulted, and the ripple effects shook institutions like Credit Suisse, Nomura, and Morgan Stanley.

The failure was not simply about poor trading. It was about the absence of **strategy–risk fusion**. Archegos pursued an aggressive strategy without risk discipline, and counterparties enabled it without aligning exposure to their stated appetites. The collapse revealed the cost of separating strategy from risk: billions lost, reputations damaged, and governance frameworks exposed as hollow.

The Reference Point for Fusion

Boards seeking to fuse strategy and risk should look to a combination of standards and frameworks:

- **COSO ERM (2017):** the global gold standard for integrating risk with strategy and performance.
- **OECD Principles (2023, II.A):** mandate boards to oversee risk in alignment with long-term objectives.
- **ISO 31000 (2018):** defines risk as uncertainty on objectives, reinforcing the link between risk and strategy.

Together, these provide a reference architecture: define objectives, articulate risk appetite, integrate assessment into strategic choices, and report on both outcomes and exposures.

Why Companies Must Fuse Strategy and Risk

Companies that separate strategy and risk invite disaster. Strategy without risk awareness becomes blind ambition — growth at any cost, expansion without foresight, innovation without ethics. Risk management without strategy becomes defensive bureaucracy — slow, compliance-driven, and incapable of enabling opportunity.

High-impact governance demands fusion because only then can boards balance ambition with resilience. It allows leaders to seize opportunities confidently while ensuring that the company can survive shocks. It transforms governance from a backward-looking audit to a forward-looking compass.

Takeaways & Reflections

The fusion of strategy and risk is not theory. It is the practical foundation of high-impact governance. Without it, companies stumble blindly into crises. With it, they navigate uncertainty with confidence and purpose.

Reflect on these questions for your own context:

Reflection 1: Strategy with Uncertainty

When our board sets strategy, do we explicitly map the risks that could derail it, or do we treat risk as a separate conversation?

Reflection 2: Risk Appetite as Compass

Have we defined and agreed upon our organization's risk appetite, and do we use it to test major strategic decisions?

Reflection 3: Fusion in Practice

What would it look like if our risk reports and strategy discussions were integrated into one boardroom dialogue, rather than two separate agendas?

Boards that achieve strategy–risk fusion are no longer guessing in the dark. They are governing with vision and vigilance. That is the path of high-impact corporate governance.

Part II Summary – Foundations of Impact-Driven Governance

Part II built the foundations of high-impact governance by exploring the evolving role of boards, the convergence of global codes, and the standards that define good practice.

We began with **the board's new mandate**: no longer narrow guardians of financial statements, boards today are stewards of purpose, accountable to stakeholders, and shapers of culture. Singapore Airlines showed us what purpose-driven governance can achieve, while Wirecard reminded us of the cost of boards that choose appearances over truth.

We then looked at the **global baselines**. From OECD 2023 to the UK Code 2024, King IV in South Africa, ASEAN frameworks, and ISO standards, we saw a convergence around shared principles: accountability, sustainability, and transparency. Yet the future of governance is also being shaped by **consumers** — whose boycotts and collective voice now influence legitimacy as powerfully as regulators or investors.

To make the landscape practical, we mapped the **major governance standards**. From the early codes (Cadbury, SOX, King Reports) to international standards (ISO, COSO, ISSB, IIA) and key markets (US, EU, UK, Asia, GCC), boards can now navigate which references matter for their context. The guidance was simple: comply locally, benchmark globally, and aspire to the best.

Finally, we fused **strategy and risk** through COSO ERM, OECD, and ISO 31000. Archegos Capital's collapse illustrated the price of separating ambition from discipline. High-impact boards align risk appetite with strategy, making uncertainty a partner in decision-making rather than a threat.

Reflection Pause

Does our board act as steward of purpose and culture, or simply as overseer of compliance?

Are we benchmarking against the right governance codes — both local and global?

Do our strategy discussions and risk assessments exist together in one conversation, or apart in silos?

Part II left us with the building blocks. High-impact governance rests on boards that embrace purpose, frameworks that converge globally, standards that provide clarity, and strategy that fuses with risk. With these foundations, companies can govern not just for compliance, but for impact.

PART III
STRATEGY, RISK & PERFORMANCE

CHAPTER 8
Internal Controls for Impact

"Governance is the architecture of trust, and internal controls are its foundation stones."

— Ali Kasa

The Meaning of Internal Controls

When boards hear the words *internal controls*, many instinctively think of auditors, checklists, and tedious paperwork. This narrow view misses the point. Internal controls are not about bureaucracy; they are about **assurance**.

Assurance means confidence — the ability of stakeholders to trust that what they are being told is accurate, that resources are being used properly, and that risks are being managed within agreed limits. Without assurance, investors withdraw, regulators intervene, employees disengage, and consumers lose faith.

The **COSO Internal Control – Integrated Framework (2013)** defines internal control as "a process, effected by an entity's board of directors, management, and other personnel, designed to provide reasonable assurance regarding the achievement of objectives." This definition carries three vital truths: controls are processes (not paperwork), they are shaped by people (not machines), and they exist to provide reasonable assurance (not perfection).

The Concept of Integrated Internal Controls

Too often, organizations design controls in silos: finance owns financial controls, compliance owns regulatory controls, IT owns cybersecurity controls, and operations own process controls. Each works in isolation, producing reports that rarely connect.

High-impact governance requires **integrated internal controls**. Integration means connecting controls across functions so that they reinforce each other. It ensures that financial reporting, operational efficiency, legal compliance, IT security, and cultural integrity are not separate checklists but parts of a single assurance system.

Petronas, Malaysia's state-owned oil and gas company, demonstrates this integration. Its governance model connects enterprise risk management, internal audit, and compliance in a "three lines of defense" system. Rather than treating controls as barriers, Petronas embeds them into decision-making, making them enablers of both resilience and growth.

Types of Internal Control

Internal controls are often classified into three broad categories, each essential for impact-driven governance:

1. **Preventive controls** – designed to stop errors or fraud before they occur (e.g., segregation of duties, authorization requirements).
2. **Detective controls** – designed to identify problems after they occur (e.g., reconciliations, audits, monitoring reports).
3. **Corrective controls** – designed to fix problems and restore systems (e.g., backup recovery, disciplinary action, process redesign).

High-impact organizations use all three in balance. Preventive controls protect, detective controls reveal, and corrective controls restore. Together, they form a cycle of assurance.

Culture, Strategy, and Internal Controls

Internal controls cannot exist without culture. A company may have the most advanced control systems in the world, but if the culture encourages cutting corners, manipulating reports, or bypassing rules, the controls will fail. Tesco's accounting scandal revealed this truth: the pressure for short-term profit eroded integrity, and controls became meaningless.

Culture shapes whether controls are respected or ignored. When leaders override controls for convenience, employees learn that the rules don't matter. When leaders uphold them even when inconvenient, they signal that integrity is non-negotiable.

Internal controls are also inseparable from **strategy**. Strategy sets objectives, and controls ensure those objectives are achieved within defined risk appetite. A growth strategy without strong controls is reckless ambition. A cautious strategy with excessive controls may suffocate opportunity. Governance aligns the two, ensuring that ambition and assurance walk together.

Case Study: Tesco's Accounting Scandal

In 2014, Tesco, one of the world's largest retailers, admitted it had overstated its profits by £263 million. The scandal was not the result of one fraudulent act but a systemic failure of internal controls. Commercial income from suppliers was recorded prematurely, margins were overstated, and oversight was weak.

The board and audit committee relied on reports that looked polished but masked aggressive accounting practices. Internal auditors raised concerns, but controls were either ignored or overridden. The result was a collapse in investor confidence, billions wiped from market value, and a reputational crisis that took years to repair.

Tesco's failure illustrates a core truth: **controls are only as strong as the culture behind them**. When performance pressure outweighs integrity, controls become decorations — visible but meaningless.

By contrast, Petronas has shown how integrated internal controls reinforce resilience. Its governance system links risk management, internal audit, and compliance into a unified assurance model. This makes controls not obstacles but enablers of strategic continuity.

Standards and References

Boards seeking to govern internal controls for impact should ground themselves in globally recognized frameworks:

- **COSO Internal Control – Integrated Framework (2013):** the global benchmark for designing and assessing controls.
- **UK Corporate Governance Code (2024, Provision 29):** requires boards to declare and explain the effectiveness of internal controls.
- **OECD Principles (2023, V.A):** emphasize disclosure and transparency, which depend on reliable controls.
- **IIA Global Standards (2024):** define how internal audit evaluates and strengthens controls.

These standards converge on one principle: controls are not optional. They are the backbone of trust, and boards must own their effectiveness.

Takeaways & Reflections

The story of Tesco shows that when internal controls are neglected or bypassed, trust collapses. The example of Petronas shows that when controls are embedded into culture and strategy, they enable resilience. Internal controls are not bureaucracy; they are the foundation of assurance and the architecture of trust.

Reflection 1: Assurance and Trust

How confident am I that our internal controls provide reasonable assurance — not just compliance — that strategy and risk are aligned with performance?

Reflection 2: Integration Across Functions

Are our internal controls siloed by department, or do they form an integrated system that connects finance, operations, compliance, and culture?

Reflection 3: Culture and Leadership

What signals do our leaders send about controls? Do they model respect for them, or do they override them when inconvenient?

Reflection 4: Controls and Strategy

When we discuss strategy, do we simultaneously test whether our internal controls and risk appetite can support it?

Internal controls will never make headlines when they work, but their absence will. Boards that govern for impact understand this paradox: controls are invisible when strong, and devastatingly visible when weak. High-impact governance ensures they are designed, embedded, respected, and constantly improve.

CHAPTER 9
Governing for Performance

"The purpose of governance is not to avoid failure, but to enable sustained performance with integrity."

— ALI KASA

What Does Performance Mean in Governance?

Performance is often confused with results. Companies report quarterly profits, growth figures, or market share, and declare success. But true performance is deeper. It is not just what numbers appear on financial statements, but whether those results are **sustainable, ethical, and aligned with purpose**.

In governance, performance means **the capacity of an organization to deliver on its strategy, honor its commitments, and endure over time**. It is about execution with discipline. Boards must therefore govern not only to measure outcomes but to ensure that performance is built on foundations that will last.

The Myth of Short-Term Performance

Many of the greatest governance failures in history were not caused by incompetence, but by the pursuit of short-term performance at the expense of long-term health. Enron delivered impressive profits — until they were revealed as lies. Lehman Brothers seemed highly profitable — until its risk exposure imploded. Tesco hit aggressive targets — until accounting irregularities destroyed trust.

Short-term performance dazzles, but it often hides fragility. High-impact governance demands that boards ask: *is this performance sustainable, or is it borrowed from the future?*

Case Study: Toyota – The Discipline of Long-Term Performance

Toyota provides one of the strongest examples of governing for performance with integrity. For decades, the company has built its governance model around long-term value creation rather than quarterly pressure.

Toyota's board emphasizes continuous improvement (*kaizen*), employee empowerment, and relentless quality standards. It invests heavily in R&D, often sacrificing short-term profit margins to secure future competitiveness. For example, Toyota began investing in hybrid technology in the 1990s, long before electric vehicles were mainstream. At the time, many analysts criticized the costs. Today, Toyota is recognized as a global leader in sustainable mobility.

This long-term orientation has paid dividends. Toyota consistently ranks among the world's most trusted automakers, has weathered crises from recalls to natural disasters, and remains financially resilient. Its governance system aligns board oversight, executive incentives, and corporate culture with sustainable performance.

Contrast this with companies that chased quarterly gains through cost-cutting or aggressive accounting, only to collapse when trust evaporated. Toyota shows that **true performance is not speed, but stamina.**

The Board's Role in Governing Performance

How can boards ensure performance is real, sustainable, and aligned with purpose? High-impact governance requires boards to oversee performance in three dimensions:

1. **Alignment with Strategy** – Boards must test whether reported performance actually supports strategic objectives. Meeting quarterly earnings targets means little if the company is drifting from its long-term vision.
2. **Integration of Risk** – Performance must always be viewed through the lens of risk appetite. A company that beats earnings by taking risks far beyond appetite is not creating value but gambling with trust.
3. **Balance of Metrics** – Financial indicators alone are insufficient. Boards must govern performance across financial, operational, cultural, and ESG dimensions. The **balanced scorecard** remains a powerful tool: financial, customer, internal processes, learning and growth.

Boards must therefore move from **passive reviewers of reports** to **active shapers of performance systems**.

Sustainable Performance Systems

High-impact governance requires that boards do more than review dashboards — they must shape **performance systems that are sustainable over time**. A sustainable performance system is one that balances short-term results with long-term value creation. It is designed to measure, reward, and reinforce outcomes that strengthen the company's purpose and resilience.

This means moving beyond narrow financial metrics to a holistic approach that includes:

- **Financial performance** — ensuring profitability and efficient use of capital.
- **Operational performance** — efficiency, innovation, and execution discipline.

- **Cultural performance** — integrity, inclusion, and employee engagement.
- **ESG and sustainability performance** — environmental stewardship, social responsibility, and ethical governance.

Sustainable systems are not static. They evolve as risks, markets, and societal expectations change. Boards must regularly test whether the measures they use still reflect what truly matters. A company that once prized growth at all costs may need to recalibrate toward resilience and stakeholder trust.

The role of governance is to ensure that **performance systems do not reward behaviors that undermine long-term value**. When incentives encourage reckless growth, compliance shortcuts, or cultural erosion, boards must intervene. Sustainable performance systems instead create alignment — where the pursuit of profit reinforces purpose, resilience, and legitimacy in society.

Performance and Incentives

Performance is shaped not only by systems but by incentives. If executives are rewarded for short-term earnings, they will chase them. If bonuses are tied to long-term sustainability, innovation, and culture, they will invest accordingly.

High-impact governance requires boards to design **executive compensation systems that align incentives with purpose and resilience**. This is where governance often fails: rewarding short-termism while preaching long-term vision. Toyota's system — which links performance incentives to quality, innovation, and market leadership, not just immediate profit — demonstrates how alignment works.

Standards and References

Boards can draw on several global frameworks when governing for performance:

- **OECD Principles (2023, II.A & V.A)**: emphasize long-term stewardship, disclosure, and accountability for performance.
- **UK Corporate Governance Code (2024, Section 1)**: requires boards to promote long-term sustainable success.
- **King IV (South Africa)**: uniquely frames governance outcomes as ethical culture, good performance, effective control, and legitimacy.
- **IIRC/ISSB Integrated Reporting Framework**: guides boards to report not just on financials, but on value creation across capitals — financial, human, intellectual, natural, and social.

These frameworks converge on a single principle: performance must be sustainable, not superficial.

The Link Between Governance and Performance

Governance and performance are often presented as opposites — governance as bureaucracy, performance as action. But the truth is that **governance is the architecture that makes performance possible.** Without governance, performance is luck; with governance, performance is discipline.

Governance sets the purpose, risk boundaries, and cultural norms that determine whether performance is real. It ensures accountability, transparency, and ethical execution. High-impact governance transforms performance from a quarterly event into a long-term legacy.

Takeaways & Reflections

Performance without governance is fragile. Governance without performance is empty. The board's role is to fuse the two into a system that creates sustainable results with integrity.

Reflect on these questions in your own context:

Reflection 1: Defining Performance

How does our board define performance? Do we see it only as financial results, or do we include culture, sustainability, and long-term resilience?

_____

_____

_____

Reflection 2: Incentives and Integrity

Do our executive compensation systems encourage long-term value creation, or do they reward short-term gains at the cost of sustainability?

_____

_____

_____

Reflection 3: Governance as Enabler

How does our governance system enable performance — not by restricting ambition, but by ensuring it is achieved with discipline, trust, and integrity?

_____

_____

_____

Closing Thought

Toyota teaches us that performance is not measured in quarterly peaks but in decades of resilience, trust, and leadership. Governance, when designed for impact, does not slow performance down — it gives it roots, discipline, and credibility. In the end, performance without governance fades, but performance with governance endures.

CHAPTER 10
Measuring What Matters

"If boards measure only profit, they will get profit — and nothing else. If they measure purpose, trust, and impact, they will get performance that endures."

— ALI KASA

Why Measurement Matters

Boards cannot govern what they do not measure. Yet the danger lies in measuring the wrong things. For too long, organizations equated performance with financial results alone: revenue, profit, shareholder return. These metrics matter — but on their own, they produce a narrow, fragile view of success.

High-impact governance insists that boards measure what matters most: not only financial outcomes, but also the health of culture, the resilience of systems, the sustainability of operations, and the trust of stakeholders. Numbers must reflect purpose, not just profit.

The Evolution of Corporate Measurement

Historically, corporate reporting was confined to financial accounts. The **Great Depression of the 1930s** gave rise to financial disclosure laws, and by the mid-20th century, accounting standards like **GAAP** and **IFRS** created global rules for profit measurement. But governance failures revealed the limits of financial focus.

In the 1990s, Kaplan and Norton introduced the **Balanced Scorecard**, which expanded measurement to four dimensions: financial, customer, internal processes, and learning & growth. This became a turning point, reminding boards that strategy execution required more than accounting.

Today, the movement has gone further. Integrated reporting, ESG metrics, and stakeholder value frameworks challenge boards to define and disclose how they create long-term value. The **OECD Principles (2023)** and **UK Code (2024)** explicitly require boards to measure sustainability and resilience, while the **ISSB IFRS S1/S2 standards** set the baseline for climate and sustainability disclosures.

The message is clear: financial performance is necessary, but no longer sufficient.

Case Study: ExxonMobil vs. India's BRSR Framework

ExxonMobil has long been criticized for resisting climate disclosure. For years, its governance focused narrowly on reserves, production, and shareholder returns, while downplaying climate risks. This blind spot eroded trust, provoked shareholder activism, and led to reputational damage. In 2021, activist investors succeeded in replacing members of Exxon's board to force greater climate accountability. The lesson: when boards refuse to measure what society demands, society finds ways to intervene.

In contrast, India introduced the **Business Responsibility and Sustainability Reporting (BRSR)** framework in 2021, making it mandatory for top-listed companies to disclose ESG performance. This reporting standard forces boards to integrate sustainability metrics — emissions, social impact, diversity — alongside financial results. Early adopters in India are already seeing benefits in investor confidence and global competitiveness.

Together, these cases show two sides of the same coin: **measurement can either erode legitimacy or strengthen it.**

The Board's Role: Choosing What to Measure

High-impact boards must make deliberate choices about what they measure. The question is not simply *what is easy to measure?* but *what matters most for our purpose and resilience?*

1. **Financial Outcomes**: Profitability, capital efficiency, growth. Still essential, but only one part of the picture.
2. **Operational Excellence**: Productivity, innovation, customer satisfaction, supply chain resilience.
3. **Culture and People**: Employee engagement, ethical behavior, diversity, psychological safety.
4. **Sustainability and ESG**: Emissions, energy use, community impact, governance practices.
5. **Trust and Reputation**: Brand value, stakeholder surveys, regulatory confidence.

The role of governance is to ensure these dimensions are measured consistently, transparently, and aligned with strategy and risk appetite.

The Balanced Scorecard: From Profit to Health

In 1992, Robert Kaplan and David Norton introduced the **Balanced Scorecard**, a breakthrough in performance governance. Their insight was simple but transformative: if organizations measure only financial results, they will optimize for profit at the expense of future health. To endure, boards must measure a balance of perspectives that together reflect the overall vitality of the company.

The Balanced Scorecard identified four dimensions:

- **Financial Perspective** – the traditional view: profitability, shareholder value, capital efficiency.
- **Customer Perspective** – measuring customer satisfaction, loyalty, and market trust.
- **Internal Process Perspective** – assessing the efficiency and quality of processes that deliver value.
- **Learning & Growth Perspective** – evaluating the health of people, culture, and innovation capacity.

By linking these perspectives into a strategy map, the Balanced Scorecard enabled boards and executives to see performance as an ecosystem rather than a single number. It created a language for strategy execution, helping organizations translate vision into measurable outcomes.

For boards today, the Balanced Scorecard remains a powerful governance tool. It transcends short-term profit and forces directors to ask: *are we investing in the future, nurturing culture, delighting customers, and building resilience — or are we merely harvesting numbers?*

In practice, high-impact boards often adapt the Balanced Scorecard to include **ESG and sustainability metrics**, making it not just balanced but holistic. This evolution ensures that governance keeps pace with society's expectations.

Integrated Reporting and Value Creation

The **International Integrated Reporting Council (IIRC)** introduced a framework that shifted boards from reporting on profit to reporting on value creation across six capitals: financial, manufactured, intellectual, human, social, and natural. Now integrated into the **ISSB standards**, this framework is increasingly global.

Integrated reporting forces boards to answer not just "what did we earn?" but "how did we create value, and at what cost to society and the environment?" It requires connectivity — showing how strategy, governance, risk, and performance are linked.

Boards that embrace integrated reporting often discover blind spots: resource depletion hidden by financial profits, cultural weakness masked by operational success, or reputational risk overlooked in quarterly results. Measurement uncovers truth.

The Future of Measurement: Impact-Weighted Accounts

The future of governance measurement lies in **impact-weighted accounts** — financial statements that reflect not only revenue and costs, but the environmental and social impact of operations. Harvard Business School's Impact-Weighted Accounts Initiative is leading this movement, and investors are watching.

Imagine two companies with identical profits, but one pollutes rivers while the other invests in clean energy. Traditional reporting treats them as equals. Impact-weighted accounts would not. Boards that fail to prepare for this shift may find themselves obsolete in the eyes of investors, regulators, and consumers.

Takeaways & Reflections

The lesson is simple: what boards choose to measure signals what they value. If they measure only profit, they may gain profit but lose legitimacy. If they measure purpose, trust, culture, and sustainability, they gain performance that endures.

Reflect on these questions:

Reflection 1: Defining Metrics

What metrics dominate our boardroom discussions? Are they financial alone, or do they reflect culture, resilience, and sustainability?

Reflection 2: Balanced View

Does our board use a balanced view of performance — financial, customer, internal, learning & growth — or are we dominated by financial dashboards?

Reflection 3: Measuring Trust

How does our board measure trust — among employees, customers, investors, and society — and what do those measures tell us about our legitimacy?

Reflection 4: Preparing for the Future

Are we ready for integrated reporting, ESG disclosure, and impact-weighted accounts, or are we still managing by outdated financial-only dashboards?

Closing Thought

Measurement is governance in action. It is the moment when purpose becomes practice, when promises become proof. Boards that measure what matters shape organizations that endure. Those that measure the wrong things may find that their numbers look good — until trust disappears and value collapses.

CHAPTER 11
Building Resilience into Strategy

"Resilience is not about avoiding storms, but about learning to sail through them without losing your course."

— Ali Kasa

Why Resilience Matters

Strategy without resilience is fragile. The past two decades have proven this truth again and again: 9/11, the 2008 financial crisis, the COVID-19 pandemic, the war in Ukraine, supply chain shocks, cyberattacks, and climate disasters. Each revealed the same reality: companies that built resilience survived and adapted, while those that prioritized only efficiency and short-term gains faltered or collapsed.

Resilience is not the absence of risk. It is the **capacity of an organization to absorb shocks, adapt quickly, and continue creating value even under pressure**. For boards, resilience is not optional — it is governance in practice.

What Is Strategic Resilience?

Strategic resilience is different from operational resilience. Operational resilience ensures continuity of processes. Strategic resilience ensures continuity of **purpose, direction, and competitive advantage**.

It is the ability of a board and executive team to adapt strategy when conditions change — without losing sight of long-term purpose. It requires foresight (anticipating risks), flexibility (adapting plans), and fortitude (making tough decisions under stress).

Resilience is not about surviving one crisis. It is about building an organization that thrives across multiple cycles of disruption.

Case Study: DBS Bank – Resilience Through Digital Transformation

DBS Bank in Singapore was once a slow-moving state-owned bank with a reputation for bureaucracy. In the mid-2000s, under CEO Piyush Gupta and with strong board support, DBS began investing heavily in digital transformation. The board viewed technology not as a cost but as a strategic resilience lever.

When COVID-19 hit in 2020, DBS was ready. With robust digital banking infrastructure, it transitioned customers and employees seamlessly to remote platforms. While many banks struggled, DBS expanded services, won global awards for innovation, and became one of the most resilient banks in Asia.

The lesson is clear: **resilience is not built during a crisis — it is built before it.** DBS invested early, and its governance enabled the foresight and discipline required to prepare for disruption.

Contrast this with Kodak, once a global leader in photography. Its board failed to adapt to digital disruption, clinging to film revenue even as technology shifted. Kodak declared bankruptcy in 2012, not because it lacked resources, but because it lacked strategic resilience.

The Board's Role in Building Resilience

Resilience is not a function for risk managers alone — it is a board-level responsibility. High-impact boards embed resilience into their oversight and leadership by focusing on:

1. **Foresight and Scenario Planning:** Boards must move beyond static budgets and ask: *what if?* They should oversee scenario analyses that test strategy against geopolitical conflict, cyberattacks, pandemics, regulatory shocks, or climate events. Good boards demand playbooks for extreme but plausible scenarios.
2. **Supply Chain and Ecosystem Oversight:** COVID-19 proved that supply chains are governance issues. Boards must monitor supplier concentration, geopolitical risks, and ethical sourcing. Resilient strategy means designing ecosystems that can flex, not break.
3. **Technology and Cybersecurity:** In the digital era, resilience depends on technology. Boards must ensure investment in cybersecurity, digital transformation, and business continuity systems. DBS Bank's resilience was built on years of board-backed tech investment.
4. **Succession and Leadership Resilience:** A company is only as resilient as its leaders. Boards must plan for CEO succession and ensure a pipeline of capable executives who can lead in crises. Without leadership resilience, no system will hold.
5. **Crisis Communication and Trust:** When crises hit, stakeholders look to boards for transparency and reassurance. Boards must insist on clear crisis communication strategies — to investors, employees, regulators, and communities. Silence erodes trust; openness builds it.
6. **Investment Trade-offs:** Resilience often requires sacrificing short-term gains for long-term stability — e.g., building redundant

capacity, diversifying suppliers, or investing in green energy. Boards must have the courage to support such trade-offs.

By taking these roles seriously, boards turn resilience from a buzzword into a lived practice.

Standards and References

Boards don't have to start from scratch. Multiple global frameworks provide guidance on embedding resilience into governance:

- **COSO ERM (2017):** Links risk management directly to strategy and performance. It encourages boards to define risk appetite, align it with strategy, and regularly review resilience to disruptions.
- **OECD Principles (2023, I & II):** Explicitly recognize resilience and sustainability as board responsibilities, requiring directors to balance shareholder and stakeholder interests over the long term.
- **ISO 22301 (Business Continuity Management):** Provides practical processes for identifying critical activities, planning for disruption, and testing continuity. Boards can require management to certify against ISO 22301 to strengthen resilience.
- **King IV (South Africa):** Frames resilience as an outcome of integrated thinking — encouraging boards to consider how financial, social, environmental, and cultural factors interact to sustain value creation.
- **UK Corporate Governance Code (2024, Section 1):** Emphasizes sustainable success, requiring boards to explain how resilience is embedded into strategy and risk oversight.

Together, these frameworks converge on a critical truth: **resilience is not separate from governance — it is governance in practice.**

Resilience and Stakeholder Trust

Resilience is not only internal. It is also about external trust. Companies that demonstrate resilience in crises strengthen relationships with investors, employees, customers, and regulators. When stakeholders see that a company can adapt while staying true to its values, trust deepens.

Conversely, companies that collapse in crises lose not just market value but legitimacy. Governance for resilience is therefore, governance for trust.

Takeaways & Reflections

Resilience is not built overnight. It is the product of foresight, preparation, culture, and governance discipline. Boards that make resilience a strategic priority create organizations capable of thriving in disruption, not merely surviving it.

Reflect on these questions in your own context:

Reflection 1: Foresight

Has our board tested strategy against multiple disruption scenarios? What blind spots remain?

Reflection 2: Investment in Resilience

Are we willing to sacrifice short-term earnings to invest in resilience — digital systems, supply chains, leadership, and culture?

Reflection 3: Learning Culture

How well does our organization learn from crises? Do we conduct reviews, and do those lessons meaningfully change our governance and strategy?

Reflection 4: Standards Alignment

Which frameworks (COSO ERM, OECD, ISO 22301, King IV, UK Code) guide our resilience planning today, and where do we fall short?

Closing Thought

Resilience is not about predicting the next crisis, but about being prepared for any crisis. Boards that embed resilience into strategy do not merely defend against shocks; they transform them into opportunities. High-impact governance ensures that when the storm comes, the company does not break — it bends, adapts, and continues to move forward with purpose.

Part III Summary – Strategy, Risk & Performance

Performance without strategy is directionless. Strategy without risk is reckless. Risk without resilience is fragile. In Part III, we explored how high-impact governance integrates all three — strategy, risk, and performance — into a system that delivers results with integrity and endurance.

We began with **internal controls**. Too often dismissed as bureaucratic, we reframed them as the backbone of trust. Tesco's accounting scandal showed what happens when controls are ignored, while Petronas demonstrated how integrated controls across functions create assurance and resilience. We also saw that controls are not just policies but culture in action, aligning strategy, risk, and accountability.

We then turned to performance governance. Toyota's long-term orientation illustrated how true performance is not speed but stamina. Boards must move from passive reviewers of reports to active shapers of sustainable performance systems. By aligning incentives, adopting frameworks like the Balanced Scorecard, and measuring more than profits, boards can ensure that performance strengthens purpose rather than undermines it.

In **measuring what matters**, we saw that what boards choose to measure signals what they value. ExxonMobil's resistance to climate disclosure contrasted sharply with India's BRSR framework, revealing that measurement can either erode legitimacy or build it. Integrated reporting, ESG metrics, and the emerging movement of impact-weighted accounts remind us that boards must look beyond financials to capture culture, sustainability, and trust.

Finally, we examined **resilience**. Through DBS Bank's digital transformation and Kodak's failure, we saw that resilience is not built in crisis but before it. High-impact boards anticipate disruption, oversee supply chains, ensure leadership succession, invest in technology, and balance short-term trade-offs with long-term survival. Standards like COSO ERM, OECD Principles, ISO 22301, King IV, and the UK Code provide a clear roadmap for embedding resilience into governance.

Reflection Pause

Are our internal controls alive in culture, or do they exist mainly on paper?

___
___
___
___

Do we govern for sustainable performance, or are we seduced by short-term metrics?

___
___
___
___

Have we defined what truly matters to measure, and does it reflect our purpose and stakeholders?

___
___
___

How resilient is our strategy to disruption — and how prepared is our board to lead through crisis?

Part III left us with this truth: governance is not just about setting direction but ensuring organizations stay on course. By embedding controls, aligning performance with purpose, measuring what truly matters, and building resilience, boards can govern for impact — delivering not only profit, but legacy.

PART IV
INTEGRITY, COMPLIANCE & CULTURE

CHAPTER 12
The Heart of Governance – Integrity in Action

"Integrity is not a policy on the wall. It is the courage to do the right thing, especially when no one is watching and when it costs the most."

— Ali Kasa

Why Integrity Is the Heart of Governance

Governance structures, codes, and processes can create order, but without integrity they collapse into empty rituals. Integrity is the moral compass of an organization, the unseen force that transforms rules into behavior and principles into practice. It is the difference between governance that looks good on paper and governance that works in reality.

High-impact governance is impossible without integrity. Boards can establish policies, but if directors and executives lack the courage to make ethical choices, governance becomes a façade. Integrity is not simply avoiding misconduct; it is actively choosing what is right, even when it is costly or unpopular.

Case Study: Siemens vs. Johnson & Johnson

In the mid-2000s, Siemens, the German engineering giant, was rocked by one of the largest corporate bribery scandals in history. Investigations revealed that the company had systematically paid bribes to secure contracts across multiple countries. While Siemens had codes of conduct and compliance policies, they were ignored or undermined by a culture where winning contracts mattered more than integrity. The company eventually paid over $1.6 billion in fines, and its reputation was severely damaged.

Contrast this with Johnson & Johnson's response to the 1982 Tylenol crisis in the United States. When cyanide-laced capsules killed several people, the company's board and executives immediately recalled 31 million bottles of Tylenol, despite enormous financial loss. Their actions were guided not by regulation but by the company's credo, which prioritized consumer safety over profit. This decision preserved public trust and became a benchmark for integrity in crisis response.

The lessons are stark: Siemens had rules without integrity, while Johnson & Johnson demonstrated integrity beyond rules. One lost legitimacy; the other strengthened it.

The Board's Role in Driving Integrity

Integrity starts with the board. Directors set the tone, and their choices shape the ethical climate of the entire organization. Boards foster integrity by:

- **Modeling Behavior:** Directors must embody the values they expect from others. If board members exploit loopholes or tolerate misconduct, the message to employees is clear: integrity is optional.
- **Embedding Purpose:** Integrity is sustained when corporate purpose and values are woven into decision-making, not treated as slogans.
- **Demanding Transparency:** Boards must insist on open disclosure of risks, challenges, and failures. Integrity thrives in sunlight but withers in secrecy.

- **Holding Executives Accountable:** Boards must ensure that leaders are evaluated not only on performance metrics but also on how they achieve them.

High-impact boards recognize that integrity cannot be delegated. It must be lived, demanded, and reinforced from the top.

Standards and References

Global governance standards consistently elevate integrity as a core principle:

- **OECD Principles (2023, Chapter II):** emphasize the need for boards to ensure ethical business conduct and accountability to stakeholders.
- **King IV (South Africa):** identifies "ethical culture" as the first governance outcome, making integrity the foundation of legitimacy.
- **UK Corporate Governance Code (2024):** requires boards to establish company purpose, values, and strategy — and ensure they are aligned with culture and decision-making.
- **ISO 37000 (Governance of Organizations):** highlights integrity and accountability as universal governance principles, applicable across sectors.

These frameworks remind boards that while compliance can be legislated, integrity must be cultivated.

Integrity and Corporate Culture

Integrity is not a document — it is culture in action. A culture of integrity means that employees feel empowered to raise concerns, refuse unethical shortcuts, and make decisions aligned with values. Conversely, when culture rewards only results, integrity becomes the first casualty.

Boards must therefore view culture as the transmission mechanism of integrity. They should demand regular assessments of whether values are alive in daily practice: through employee surveys, whistleblowing channels, and boardroom discussions that prioritize ethics over expedience.

Takeaways & Reflections

Integrity is the beating heart of governance. Without it, codes and controls are hollow. With it, organizations earn trust, legitimacy, and resilience.

Reflect on these questions for your boardroom:

Reflection 1: Tone from the Top

Do our board members and executives consistently model integrity, even when it is costly or inconvenient?

_____

_____

_____

_____

Reflection 2: Integrity in Practice

Are our purpose and values embedded in real decisions, or are they mostly words on posters and websites?

_____

_____

_____

_____

Reflection 3: Culture of Integrity

How does our organization reinforce integrity in daily operations — through recognition, accountability, and openness to speak up?

_____

_____

_____

_____

Closing Thought

Integrity cannot be outsourced, automated, or mandated by regulation. It must be chosen, modeled, and defended every day. Boards that lead with integrity create organizations that not only perform but endure. Governance without integrity is an empty shell; governance with integrity is a living system that earns trust and legitimacy.

CHAPTER 13
Compliance as Enabler, Not Burden

"Compliance is not the enemy of performance. It is the framework that makes performance legitimate."

— ALI KASA

The Misunderstanding of Compliance

For many boards and executives, the word *compliance* evokes frustration. It is seen as a cost center, a distraction from "real business," or a burden imposed by regulators. In this mindset, compliance becomes a **box-ticking exercise**: forms to file, checklists to complete, audits to endure.

But high-impact governance reframes compliance. Compliance is not about slowing companies down — it is about **keeping them on the track of trust**. Done well, compliance does not stifle ambition; it protects and amplifies it. It ensures that growth is sustainable, that performance is defensible, and that reputation is preserved.

Case Study: Volkswagen Dieselgate – The Cost of Compliance Failure

In 2015, Volkswagen was exposed for installing software in millions of cars that cheated emissions tests. The company had sophisticated compliance systems on paper, but the culture treated compliance as an obstacle to be bypassed. Engineers were pressured to meet unrealistic performance targets, and management overlooked ethical concerns.

The result: over $30 billion in fines, legal settlements, and reputational damage that still lingers today. The scandal revealed a simple truth: **compliance ignored is far more expensive than compliance embraced.**

Volkswagen's failure stands as a warning. Compliance treated as a burden breeds shortcuts, deception, and systemic failure. Compliance treated as an enabler preserves legitimacy and long-term value.

Compliance as Strategic Advantage

High-impact organizations view compliance as a **strategic advantage**, not just a defensive shield. For example:

- **Data protection compliance (GDPR):** builds consumer trust in how companies handle personal information.
- **Anti-bribery compliance (ISO 37001):** reassures investors and partners in global markets.
- **Sustainability compliance (ISSB standards, CSRD in Europe):** signals resilience and attracts ESG-focused capital.

In each case, compliance is not merely about avoiding penalties; it is about signaling trustworthiness, opening doors to markets, and securing long-term competitiveness.

From "Comply or Explain" to "Apply and Evidence"

Traditional corporate governance codes often follow the principle of *"comply or explain."* Companies are allowed to deviate from rules if they disclose why. While flexible, this has sometimes encouraged minimal compliance — explanations without substance.

The new trend is toward *"apply and evidence."* Regulators and investors increasingly expect companies not only to adopt standards but to **prove through evidence** that they are applied in practice. Boards must therefore move beyond reporting compliance to demonstrating it — through audits, independent assurance, and transparent disclosure.

This shift strengthens governance credibility: what is claimed must be shown.

Standards and References

Boards can leverage multiple frameworks to embed compliance as value creation:

- **OECD Principles (2023, V.A)**: stress transparency and accountability, which depend on strong compliance structures.
- **ISO 37301 (Compliance Management Systems)**: provides a certifiable global standard for designing, implementing, and evaluating compliance systems.
- **ISO 37001 (Anti-Bribery Management Systems)**: offers tools to prevent, detect, and respond to bribery risks.
- **UK Corporate Governance Code (2024)**: integrates compliance into board accountability for risk and culture.
- **IIA Standards (2024)**: require internal auditors to provide assurance on compliance effectiveness.

These frameworks guide boards to treat compliance not as minimum legal conformity, but as a strategic driver of integrity and performance.

The Board's Role in Compliance

Boards must elevate compliance from a department to a culture. Their role includes:

- **Oversight**: ensuring the compliance function has independence, resources, and authority.
- **Integration**: embedding compliance into strategy, operations, and risk appetite.

- **Monitoring**: reviewing compliance dashboards and demanding evidence, not just assurance.
- **Accountability**: holding executives responsible for breaches, not just frontline staff.
- **Culture-setting**: signaling that compliance is not negotiable — it is part of how the company competes.

Boards that lead in this way transform compliance from a drag on performance into the invisible shield that sustains it.

Takeaways & Reflections

Compliance is not the opposite of ambition; it is the condition that makes ambition possible. The cost of neglect is far higher than the cost of doing it right.

Reflect on these questions in your own context:

Reflection 1: Compliance Mindset

Do we view compliance in our organization as a burden or as an enabler of trust and competitiveness?

Reflection 2: Evidence of Compliance

When our board receives compliance reports, do we ask for evidence of application, or are we satisfied with checklists and assurances?

Reflection 3: Compliance and Culture

What message do our leaders send about compliance? Is it treated as optional when inconvenient, or as integral to strategy and values?

Closing Thought

Compliance is not about slowing down companies. It is about ensuring they go faster without derailing. Boards that embrace compliance as an enabler safeguard legitimacy, protect performance, and position their organizations for sustainable success

CHAPTER 14
Culture – The Invisible Hand of Governance

"Culture is not what we write in manuals. It is what people do when no one is watching, and what leaders allow when the pressure is on."

— ALI KASA

Why Culture Governs Governance

Every boardroom can adopt codes, frameworks, and compliance systems. But whether those systems succeed depends on one invisible force: culture. Culture is the collective set of values, assumptions, and behaviors that define how people act.

As management thinker Peter Drucker famously noted, *"Culture eats strategy for breakfast."* The same is true for governance. The most sophisticated risk frameworks, compliance policies, or performance dashboards will collapse if the organizational culture rewards shortcuts, tolerates silence, or celebrates results over integrity.

Culture is the invisible hand of governance: shaping decisions, guiding actions, and silently defining what is acceptable.

Case Study: Wells Fargo – When Culture Destroys Trust

For years, Wells Fargo was celebrated as one of America's most admired banks. Yet between 2002 and 2016, its culture eroded into a toxic obsession with sales targets. Employees, under extreme pressure to "cross-sell" products, created millions of fake accounts without customer consent.

The scandal revealed a culture where meeting targets took precedence over honesty. Compliance systems existed, but they were ignored or manipulated. The board failed to recognize how performance incentives were eroding the culture. The result was billions in fines, the resignation of senior leaders, and a catastrophic loss of trust.

Wells Fargo's failure was not technical — it was cultural. The wrong values had been rewarded for too long.

The Board's Role in Governing Culture

Boards cannot directly manage culture, but they can shape, monitor, and reinforce it. Their responsibilities include:

1. **Defining Desired Culture:** Boards must ensure that the organization has a clearly articulated purpose and values, communicated consistently across all levels.
2. **Aligning Incentives:** Culture is shaped by what gets rewarded. Boards must oversee executive compensation and performance systems to ensure they encourage ethical, sustainable behavior rather than reckless targets.
3. **Monitoring Signals:** Boards must demand regular reporting on cultural health: employee engagement surveys, whistleblower reports, turnover data, and ethical breaches.
4. **Creating Safe Speak-Up Channels:** Employees should feel empowered to raise concerns without fear. Boards must oversee

whistleblowing and grievance systems and ensure independence and protection.
5. **Holding Leaders Accountable:** Culture is modeled at the top. Boards must remove leaders who undermine integrity, even if they deliver financial performance.

When boards treat culture as central, governance gains life. When they ignore it, governance collapses into paperwork.

Standards and References

Culture is gaining recognition in global governance standards:

- **UK Corporate Governance Code (2024, Provision 2)**: requires boards to monitor and assess company culture, ensuring alignment with purpose and values.
- **OECD Principles (2023, II.B)**: emphasize the role of boards in overseeing ethical conduct and culture.
- **King IV (South Africa)**: uniquely identifies ethical culture as the first governance outcome — the root of trust and legitimacy.
- **ISO 37000 (Governance of Organizations)**: stresses culture as a principle guiding accountability, fairness, and transparency.

These frameworks converge on a clear message: boards must treat culture as a measurable and governable asset, not a vague abstraction.

Culture as Risk and Opportunity

Culture can be the greatest risk — or the greatest enabler. A toxic culture multiplies misconduct, as seen at Wells Fargo. A strong culture multiplies trust and resilience. For example, companies like **Patagonia** and **Unilever** have built cultures that empower employees to live values of sustainability and purpose, creating not just compliance but competitive advantage.

Boards must see culture not only as a soft risk but as a hard driver of performance and legitimacy.

Takeaways & Reflections

Culture is the invisible hand that either supports or sabotages governance. Boards that govern for culture turn values into daily practice and prevent silent erosion.

Reflect on these questions in your own context:

Reflection 1: Values in Practice

Do our stated values show up in daily behaviors, or do employees see them as slogans disconnected from reality?

Reflection 2: Incentives and Culture

What do our reward systems encourage — sustainable behavior or short-term results at any cost?

Reflection 3: Monitoring Culture

How does our board measure and monitor culture? Are we receiving honest data, or filtered reports that hide the truth?

Reflection 4: Leadership Accountability

Have we ever removed or challenged a leader for damaging culture, even if their financial performance was strong?

Closing Thought

Culture is not optional, and it is not invisible to those who choose to see. Boards that treat culture as a serious governance priority create organizations where values are lived, trust is earned, and resilience is built. Without culture, governance is fragile. With culture, governance is unshakable.

CHAPTER 15
Ethics, Whistleblowing & Moral Courage

"The test of governance is not how well people follow rules, but how bravely they speak when rules are broken."

— ALI KASA

Why Ethics Matters Beyond Codes

Every major company today has a code of ethics. Yet scandals continue. Why? Because codes are only as strong as the culture and courage that bring them to life. Ethics is not the existence of a document — it is the daily practice of asking: *is this right?*

Governance collapses when ethical questions are replaced with legal loopholes. Laws can tell companies what is permissible. Ethics asks a deeper question: *what is right, fair, and aligned with our purpose?* Boards that confuse legality with ethics risk creating organizations that comply with the letter of the law while betraying its spirit.

Case Study: Olympus and the Whistleblower Who Spoke Up

In 2011, Michael Woodford, the British CEO of Olympus, discovered $1.7 billion in accounting irregularities hidden by the company's leadership. When he raised concerns, he was dismissed from his role and ostracized. But Woodford refused to stay silent. He blew the whistle, exposing one of Japan's largest corporate scandals.

Olympus initially tried to bury the issue, but public and regulatory pressure forced reform. Woodford's courage cost him his position, but it preserved integrity for the company and its stakeholders. His story highlights both the risks whistleblowers face and the critical role boards play in protecting them.

The lesson is clear: without protection for truth-tellers, governance is blind.

The Role of Whistleblowing in Governance

Whistleblowing is not betrayal. It is an act of loyalty to the truth, to stakeholders, and to the long-term health of the company. High-impact governance treats whistleblowing systems as essential, not optional.

Boards must ensure:

- **Safe Channels**: multiple independent reporting systems (hotlines, ombudsmen, secure digital platforms).
- **Protection from Retaliation**: clear policies and enforcement that protect whistleblowers from dismissal, harassment, or career damage.
- **Board-Level Oversight**: whistleblowing reports should reach the audit committee or a designated ethics committee, not be buried in management layers.
- **Learning from Reports**: whistleblowing must trigger investigation, root-cause analysis, and systemic reform, not just case-by-case fixes.

When whistleblowers are silenced, problems multiply. When they are protected, organizations avoid disaster.

Moral Courage: The Human Core of Governance

Ultimately, governance depends not only on systems but on people willing to act with courage. **Moral courage** is the ability to choose the right path even when it is risky, unpopular, or costly. It is what separates governance as paperwork from governance as practice.

Boards must actively cultivate moral courage by:

- **Setting Tone from the Top**: showing that speaking up is valued, not punished.
- **Recognizing Ethical Leadership**: rewarding leaders who make difficult ethical decisions, not only those who deliver numbers.
- **Creating Safe Space for Debate**: encouraging directors and executives to challenge assumptions and raise concerns.
- **Supporting Individuals Who Speak Truth**: whether whistleblowers, auditors, or employees.

As former UN Secretary-General Kofi Annan once said: *"Without good governance, without integrity and courage, no amount of laws or policies will save us."*

Standards and References

Global standards reinforce the importance of ethics and whistleblowing:

- **OECD Principles (2023, II.B)**: require boards to oversee ethical conduct and protect stakeholders who expose misconduct.
- **UK Corporate Governance Code (2024, Provision 6)**: mandates whistleblowing arrangements that allow employees to raise concerns in confidence and with protection.
- **ISO 37002 (Whistleblowing Management Systems)**: provides guidance on establishing, implementing, and maintaining effective whistleblowing frameworks.

- **King IV (South Africa)**: emphasizes moral courage, ethical leadership, and the need for an ethical culture as a governance outcome.

These standards converge on one message: ethics and courage cannot be delegated — they must be led.

Takeaways & Reflections

Ethics, whistleblowing, and moral courage are the final safety net of governance. Without them, policies fail and risks multiply. With them, organizations earn legitimacy that no scandal can easily shake.

Reflect on these questions in your own context:

Reflection 1: Beyond Legalism

Do we, as a board, ask only what is legal — or do we also ask what is ethical and aligned with our values?

Reflection 2: Whistleblowing Systems

Are our whistleblowing channels trusted, independent, and accessible to employees — or do people fear retaliation if they speak up?

Reflection 3: Moral Courage in Leadership

How do we encourage moral courage among executives and employees? Do we reward truth-tellers, or do we punish them for being inconvenient?

_____

_____

_____

Part III Summary – Integrity, Compliance & Culture

Governance without ethics is a house built on sand. Whistleblowers and courageous leaders provide the anchors of truth that prevent collapse. Boards that protect integrity, encourage moral courage, and create safe channels for speaking up are not only compliant — they are truly legitimate. High-impact governance rests on courage, because without it, even the best systems fail.

Governance lives or dies not in the boardroom papers but in the daily choices people make. Part IV showed us that high-impact governance rests on integrity, compliance, culture, and moral courage — the human and ethical foundations that give structures their strength.

We began with **integrity**. Siemens' global bribery scandal revealed that codes without integrity are hollow, while Johnson & Johnson's Tylenol recall showed how integrity beyond regulation builds trust. Integrity is not a policy; it is action — the heartbeat of governance.

We then reframed **compliance**. Volkswagen's Dieselgate scandal demonstrated the devastating cost of treating compliance as a burden. In contrast, organizations that embrace compliance as an enabler of trust, such as those adopting ISO 37301 or GDPR best practices, show that compliance is not about slowing companies down but about protecting them as they grow.

In **culture**, we saw that values unspoken shape governance more than any manual. Wells Fargo's fake accounts scandal exposed how toxic cultures corrode trust, while companies like Patagonia and Unilever show how purpose-driven cultures create resilience and advantage. Boards cannot directly manage culture, but they can define, measure, and hold leaders accountable for it.

Finally, we explored **ethics, whistleblowing, and moral courage**. Olympus whistleblower Michael Woodford showed how courage can expose truth and preserve integrity, even at great personal cost. Without safe channels and board-level protection, governance is blind. Without moral courage, even the best systems fail.

Reflection Pause

Do our leaders live integrity, or only speak of it?

___

___

Is compliance in our company a shield of trust or a box-ticking burden?

___

___

What signals does our culture send every day, and are they aligned with purpose?

___

___

Do we reward moral courage and protect whistleblowers, or do we silence them?

___

___

Part IV left us with this truth: governance is not only about systems, structures, and metrics. It is about people — their integrity, their courage, their culture, and their willingness to do what is right when it matters most. Without these foundations, governance collapses. With them, governance endures

PART V
STAKEHOLDERS, SUSTAINABILITY & ESG

CHAPTER 16
Stakeholders and the Purpose of the Corporation

"The purpose of the corporation is not to serve shareholders alone, but to create value responsibly for all those whose lives it touches."

— ALI KASA

From Shareholder Primacy to Stakeholder Governance

For most of the 20th century, corporate governance was defined by *shareholder primacy*. Boards were expected to maximize shareholder value above all else. This philosophy, popularized by economist Milton Friedman in 1970, dominated corporate thinking for decades.

Yet the world has changed. Climate risks, social inequality, digital disruption, and global crises have exposed the limitations of shareholder primacy. Companies that focus only on quarterly earnings often neglect long-term sustainability, community impact, and the trust of employees and consumers.

The shift is clear: today, governance is judged not only by how well it rewards shareholders but by how responsibly it serves **all stakeholders** — employees, customers, suppliers, regulators, communities, and the environment.

Case Study: The Business Roundtable vs. Danone

In 2019, the Business Roundtable (BRT), a group of nearly 200 CEOs of major U.S. corporations, issued a landmark statement redefining the purpose of the corporation. For the first time, they declared that companies exist to serve all stakeholders, not just shareholders. This statement was celebrated as a turning point in corporate governance.

Yet critics argued that the pledge was symbolic. Many BRT companies continued business practices that prioritized short-term shareholder returns. The gap between rhetoric and reality raised questions about whether stakeholder governance was truly embraced or merely rebranded.

Contrast this with Danone under CEO Emmanuel Faber. Danone sought to integrate stakeholder governance into its legal structure, becoming the first listed French company to adopt the "Entreprise à Mission" model — embedding purpose and social goals into its bylaws. However, despite this bold move, Faber was ousted in 2021 after shareholder pressure mounted over short-term financial performance.

The lesson from both stories is sobering: shifting from shareholder primacy to stakeholder governance requires more than words. It demands governance systems, board courage, and investor alignment. Without them, stakeholder promises risk collapse under shareholder pressure.

The Board's Role in Stakeholder Governance

High-impact boards cannot avoid the stakeholder question. Their responsibilities include:

1. **Defining Purpose:** Boards must clearly articulate the company's purpose beyond profit. Purpose guides strategy, shapes culture, and signals accountability to stakeholders.

2. **Identifying Stakeholders:** Boards should map who their stakeholders are and how their interests intersect. Employees, customers, regulators, communities, and the environment are not externalities — they are essential to legitimacy.
3. **Balancing Interests:** Governance is not about pleasing everyone equally, but about making informed, transparent trade-offs when stakeholder interests conflict. Boards must decide: whose interests prevail, and why?
4. **Embedding Stakeholder Metrics:** Boards should ensure that performance dashboards include stakeholder measures: employee engagement, customer trust, supplier sustainability, community impact.
5. **Engaging Directly:** Boards should not rely solely on management summaries. They must hear stakeholder voices directly — through site visits, town halls, advisory councils, and investor dialogues.

By embracing these responsibilities, boards transform stakeholder governance from rhetoric into reality.

Standards and References

Global standards reinforce the shift to stakeholder orientation:

- **OECD Principles (2023, II.A):** emphasize the board's duty to balance shareholder and stakeholder interests for long-term sustainability.
- **King IV (South Africa):** places stakeholders at the heart of governance, requiring integrated thinking and reporting.
- **UK Corporate Governance Code (2024, Section 1):** highlights long-term sustainable success, linking purpose and culture to stakeholder interests.

- **ISO 37000 (Governance of Organizations):** identifies "purpose" and "stakeholder engagement" as universal principles of effective governance.

These frameworks converge on a single idea: the corporation is a social institution, not just a financial machine.

Stakeholders as Risk and Opportunity

Ignoring stakeholders creates risks. Companies that disregard workers face strikes. Those that neglect customers face boycotts. Those that ignore climate face lawsuits and reputational damage.

But stakeholder engagement also creates opportunities. Companies that listen to employees attract talent. Those that align with communities gain legitimacy. Those that integrate environmental goals secure investor support. Stakeholder governance is therefore not a moral add-on; it is a strategic necessity.

Takeaways & Reflections

Stakeholder governance is not a slogan. It is the recognition that corporations exist within society, not above it. Boards that embrace this truth strengthen both legitimacy and performance.

Reflect on these questions:

Reflection 1: Defining Purpose

Has our board clearly defined the purpose of the corporation — beyond profit — and does it guide our decisions?

_____

_____

_____

Reflection 2: Stakeholder Mapping

Do we know who our key stakeholders are and how their interests intersect with our long-term strategy?

Reflection 3: Balancing Trade-Offs

When stakeholder interests conflict, how do we decide? Do we have transparent principles, or do we default to shareholder primacy?

Closing Thought

The era of shareholder primacy is fading. High-impact governance recognizes that corporations survive and thrive only when they create value for all stakeholders. Boards that embrace this reality are not diluting purpose — they are fulfilling it.

CHAPTER 17
ESG as a Governance Imperative

"ESG is not a checklist. It is how boards prove that performance is achieved with responsibility, resilience, and legitimacy."

— ALI KASA

From Optional to Imperative

A decade ago, environmental, social, and governance (ESG) issues were seen as optional. They lived in sustainability reports, far from the boardroom. Today, ESG is no longer peripheral. Investors, regulators, employees, and consumers demand that companies demonstrate how they create value responsibly.

High-impact governance treats ESG as a **core board responsibility**. It is not about glossy reports or ratings but about embedding environmental stewardship, social responsibility, and governance integrity into decision-making. ESG is the language through which boards prove they are governing not just for profit, but for legitimacy.

Case Study: ExxonMobil vs. BlackRock's Stewardship Activism

In 2021, a small activist hedge fund, Engine No. 1, launched a campaign against ExxonMobil, accusing the board of failing to prepare for the low-carbon transition. Despite owning only 0.02% of Exxon's shares, the fund secured support from institutional investors like BlackRock, Vanguard, and State Street. The result: three directors were replaced with candidates committed to climate strategy.

This was a watershed moment. Investors made clear that boards ignoring ESG — particularly climate — would face accountability at the ballot box. Exxon's resistance to climate disclosure became a case study in governance failure.

By contrast, BlackRock, the world's largest asset manager, has consistently emphasized ESG stewardship. Its annual letters to CEOs urge companies to adopt long-term sustainability strategies, disclose climate risks, and engage stakeholders. BlackRock's activism reflects the growing consensus: ESG is not philanthropy but financial stewardship.

The Board's Role in ESG Governance

Boards must lead the integration of ESG into governance. Their responsibilities include:

1. **Oversight of ESG Strategy:** Boards must ensure ESG is not siloed in sustainability teams but integrated into overall strategy and risk appetite.
2. **Disclosure and Transparency:** Boards must demand rigorous ESG disclosure, aligned with global standards, ensuring that reports reflect reality, not marketing.
3. **Investor and Stakeholder Engagement:** Boards should engage directly with investors, regulators, and communities on ESG issues, not leave it entirely to management.
4. **Link to Incentives:** Boards must align executive compensation with ESG goals — emissions reduction, diversity, safety — to ensure accountability.

5. **Continuous Learning:** ESG is evolving rapidly. Boards must commit to learning about climate science, social trends, and regulatory shifts to govern effectively.

Standards and References

The ESG landscape is complex, but key standards provide a global baseline:

- **ISSB (IFRS S1 & S2, 2023):** the new global baseline for sustainability and climate disclosure.
- **EU Corporate Sustainability Reporting Directive (CSRD):** requires detailed sustainability reporting by thousands of European companies and multinationals operating in the EU.
- **SASB Standards (now under ISSB):** provide sector-specific ESG metrics.
- **GRI Standards:** widely used for reporting on environmental and social impacts.
- **Task Force on Climate-Related Financial Disclosures (TCFD):** framework for climate risk disclosure, now integrated into ISSB S2.

Boards must ensure their companies align with these standards to remain competitive and credible.

ESG Skepticism vs. Investor Expectations

ESG has faced backlash, especially in parts of the United States where it is criticized as "politicized" or a distraction from profits. Some states have even restricted ESG-related investments.

Yet global investor trends tell a different story: ESG-focused funds continue to attract capital, and regulators worldwide are embedding sustainability into law. Boards cannot dismiss ESG as a fad. The real question is not *whether* to engage with ESG, but *how to govern it credibly.*

High-impact boards navigate the tension by focusing on materiality: identifying which ESG issues are most relevant to their industry, stakeholders, and long-term value.

ESG as Performance, Not Philanthropy

Too often, ESG is mistaken for corporate social responsibility (CSR) — charity projects, community sponsorships, or marketing campaigns. True ESG is different. It is about embedding environmental stewardship, social equity, and governance integrity into the core operating model.

For example:

- **Environmental:** reducing emissions, investing in clean energy, and building climate resilience.
- **Social:** protecting worker rights, ensuring diversity, and strengthening supply chain responsibility.
- **Governance:** ensuring board diversity, transparent reporting, and ethical leadership.

When ESG is embedded into strategy, it strengthens resilience and competitiveness. When it is treated as philanthropy, it becomes a distraction.

Takeaways & Reflections

ESG is not an add-on. It is governance in practice — the way boards prove they are creating long-term value responsibly.

Reflect on these questions:

Reflection 1: ESG Strategy

Is ESG integrated into our strategy and risk management, or is it treated as a separate report?

Reflection 2: Standards Alignment

Which ESG standards (ISSB, CSRD, SASB, GRI, TCFD) do we align with, and how confident are we in the accuracy of our disclosures?

Reflection 3: Investor Engagement

How do we as a board engage with investors and stakeholders on ESG? Do we wait for questions, or do we lead the dialogue?

Reflection 4: Incentives and Accountability

Is executive compensation linked to ESG outcomes, or are sustainability commitments disconnected from leadership rewards?

Closing Thought

ESG is not about politics or philanthropy. It is about credibility, resilience, and trust. Boards that treat ESG as a governance imperative will not only comply with regulation but earn the legitimacy that sustains performance in a changing world. Those that dismiss it risk irrelevance, activism, and collapse.

CHAPTER 18
Climate, Environment & Long-Term Governance

"Climate governance is not about saving the planet alone. It is about saving companies from irrelevance in a world that is changing faster than their strategies."

— ALI KASA

The Era of Climate Risk

For much of corporate history, environmental issues were considered externalities — costs to society, not to the company. But in today's world, climate change is no longer an external issue. It is a direct business risk.

Floods disrupt supply chains. Droughts cripple agriculture. Wildfires halt operations. New carbon regulations reshape markets. Investor expectations force disclosure. Consumer boycotts punish polluters. Insurers and lenders price climate risk into capital.

Boards that ignore climate governance risk shareholder lawsuits, regulatory fines, reputational collapse, and operational fragility. Climate is not only a sustainability issue — it is a financial, strategic, and governance issue.

Case Study: Shell and Climate Litigation

In 2021, a Dutch court ordered Royal Dutch Shell to reduce its carbon emissions by 45% by 2030, compared to 2019 levels. The case, brought by environmental groups and supported by 17,000 Dutch citizens, was the first time a company was legally required to align its strategy with the Paris Climate Agreement.

Shell argued it was already transitioning toward renewables, but the court found its commitments insufficient. The ruling sent shockwaves through boardrooms worldwide: **climate governance is no longer voluntary — it is enforceable.**

Shell's case illustrates a profound shift: climate obligations are moving from reputational expectations to legal mandates. Boards can no longer treat climate as "CSR." It is now a binding governance issue.

The Board's Role in Climate and Environmental Governance

Boards must elevate climate and environmental stewardship to the heart of governance. Key responsibilities include:

1. **Integrating Climate into Strategy:** Climate risk must be part of strategic planning, not a sustainability appendix. Boards should oversee transition strategies for decarbonization, renewable energy investment, and sustainable products.
2. **Disclosure and Transparency:** Boards must ensure climate-related disclosures align with global standards (TCFD, ISSB S2, CSRD). Reporting is not about marketing; it is about credibility with investors and regulators.
3. **Oversight of Risk and Resilience:** Climate risk should be embedded in enterprise risk management. Boards must demand stress tests, scenario analyses, and resilience plans for physical and transition risks.
4. **Stakeholder Engagement:** Boards must recognize that regulators, investors, NGOs, and consumers are all watching. Proactive engagement strengthens legitimacy.

5. **Accountability Through Incentives:** Executive compensation must be tied to climate performance — emissions reduction, energy efficiency, innovation. Without accountability, climate commitments remain empty.

Standards and References

Boards have multiple frameworks to guide climate governance:

- **Task Force on Climate-Related Financial Disclosures (TCFD):** requires boards to disclose governance, strategy, risk, and metrics for climate.
- **ISSB S2 (2023):** sets the new global baseline for climate-related disclosures, building on TCFD.
- **ISO 14001 (Environmental Management Systems):** provides a certifiable framework for managing environmental impacts across operations.
- **EU CSRD (2024 onwards):** mandates detailed climate and sustainability disclosures for European and multinational companies.
- **OECD Principles (2023, II.A & V.A):** highlight sustainability and risk as central to governance responsibilities.

Together, these standards ensure climate governance is not subjective but structured, measurable, and comparable.

Climate as Long-Term Governance

Boards must recognize that climate is not only about avoiding fines or lawsuits — it is about positioning the company for the future. As economies shift toward net-zero, companies that cling to high-carbon models will lose competitiveness, investor support, and social license to operate.

Conversely, companies that invest in climate innovation — clean energy, circular economy, sustainable products — will gain legitimacy, resilience, and access to capital. Climate governance is therefore not only defensive, but offensive: it creates long-term advantage.

Takeaways & Reflections

Climate and environmental stewardship are no longer optional extras. They are existential governance responsibilities that define whether companies endure.

Reflect on these questions:

Reflection 1: Climate Strategy

Is climate risk integrated into our corporate strategy, or is it handled as a side project in sustainability reports?

Reflection 2: Disclosure

Do our climate disclosures align with TCFD/ISSB S2 standards, and do they provide investors with credible, decision-useful information?

Reflection 3: Incentives

Is climate performance tied to executive pay and board accountability, or do commitments remain unlinked to real incentives?

Reflection 4: Future Readiness

Are we preparing our company for a net-zero economy, or are we clinging to high-carbon strategies that may soon become obsolete?

Closing Thought

Climate governance is no longer about optics. It is about survival. Boards that lead on climate will position their companies for resilience, legitimacy, and competitiveness in the decades ahead. Boards that delay will find themselves forced by courts, regulators, or markets — often too late. High-impact governance means governing for the planet and for the long-term survival of the corporation itself.

CHAPTER 19
Social Responsibility and the Consumer Voice

"In today's world, customers don't just vote with their wallets—they govern with them."

— ALI KASA

Why Social Responsibility and Consumer Voice Matter

Stakeholders beyond investors and regulators are reshaping the governance landscape. Activist consumers, organized civil society, and digital-era movements now wield the power to influence—not just public perception—but board-level decisions. Social responsibility isn't merely about branding; it's a matter of reputation, legitimacy, and societal accountability.

Consumers expect companies to act ethically and sustainably. When firms appear misaligned with public sentiment—be it through perceived inaction or complicity—they face repercussions swiftly, sometimes in real time. This dynamic shifts governance: boards must now factor in external societal pressures and foresee how consumer actions can materially affect their company.

Case Study 1: Starbucks and the Gaza War Boycott

Following perceived missteps during the Gaza conflict, Starbucks faced a wave of consumer boycotts across multiple regions. In Malaysia, where operations are franchised by Berjaya Food Bhd, Starbucks' sales plummeted

36% year-over-year, and the company posted a net loss of approximately $69 million for the financial year ending June 2025.

Additionally, Reuters reported that both Starbucks and McDonald's experienced significant sales declines in Muslim-majority regions, tracing them in part to boycott campaigns prompted by the Israel-Gaza conflict. These incidents underscore a sobering truth: brand actions—or even misperceptions—can prompt rapid consumer action with direct financial impact.

Case Study 2: B Corp Certification as Social Responsibility in Action

On the other side of social accountability, some companies proactively distinguish themselves through certification and responsible governance. Research shows that firms with **B Corp certification**—demonstrating a commitment to social and environmental purpose—experience **positive effects on turnover growth**, increasing over time as certified values resonate with stakeholders. These companies signal that social responsibility can be a competitive advantage, not just a moral stance.

The Board's Role in Navigating Consumer-Driven Governance

Boards must now adapt to a world where consumer sentiment can be both a threat and an ally. Their responsibilities include:

1. **Monitoring Public Discourse:** Boards should track social media, campaigns, and consumer sentiment that can signal emerging reputational risks.
2. **Ensuring Authentic Social Responsibility:** Efforts must go beyond marketing—social initiatives must reflect core purpose, not just optics.

3. **Proactive Engagement:** Rather than reacting endlessly to boycotts, boards should engage with community groups and consumers proactively, building trust.
4. **Policy Alignment:** Boards must ensure that commercial decisions (e.g., union policies or international partnerships) align with broader brand values to avoid backlash.
5. **Leveraging Positive Certifications:** Adopting certifications like B Corp or benefiting from verified endorsements signals long-term commitment to values, building trust with socially conscious consumers.

Standards and References

- **UN Global Compact & OECD Guidelines for Multinational Enterprises:** Guide board-level responsibility in social and consumer engagement.
- **ISO 26000 (Guidance on Social Responsibility):** A framework for organizations to operate ethically and build consumer and societal trust.
- **Benefit Corporation frameworks:** Legally enforceable commitments to broader social goals, of which B Corp certification is a widely respected seal.

These standards help anchor social responsibility in governance—not as reaction but as a structured, values-based commitment.

Takeaways & Reflections

Social responsibility is no longer discretionary—it's a strategic imperative. Whether through negative campaigns or positive certifications, consumer voice matters, and boards must be ready.

Reflection 1: Consumer Sentiments

How do we actively listen to consumer sentiment, and what governance mechanisms ensure we respond thoughtfully, not reactively?

Reflection 2: Social Backlash

Have we ever faced a consumer or social backlash? What did our board learn—and how did we adapt?

Reflection 3: B Corporation Certification

Could social responsibility certifications (e.g., B Corp) align with our purpose—and would our board support that?

Closing Thought

Consumers now act with governance power, holding companies accountable through their purchases and platforms. Boards that understand this shift—and integrate social responsibility authentically—will not only withstand backlash but gain trust, resilience, and longevity

CHAPTER 20
From ESG to Impact Governance

"The next era of governance will not ask what you reported, but what you changed."

— ALI KASA

The Limits of ESG

ESG has become the global language of sustainability. Companies now issue ESG reports, align with ISSB or GRI standards, and engage investors on sustainability metrics. This is progress. Yet, ESG also faces criticism:

- **Box-Ticking:** Some companies treat ESG as compliance, producing glossy reports without changing core business models.
- **Inconsistency:** With multiple standards and ratings, ESG scores often vary widely for the same company, confusing investors.
- **Greenwashing Risks**: Without robust verification, ESG reporting can exaggerate claims and undermine trust.

ESG is necessary, but it is not sufficient. The next frontier is **impact governance** — governance that measures and manages how companies actually change the world.

What Is Impact Governance?

Impact governance is the discipline of ensuring that boards oversee not only the disclosure of ESG data but the **real-world outcomes** of corporate actions. It asks:

- Did emissions actually decrease, or were they offset on paper?
- Did diversity programs create inclusion, or just improve statistics?
- Did community investments improve lives, or merely enhance reputation?

Impact governance moves the conversation from **inputs and outputs** to **outcomes and impact**. It redefines performance to include not only financial returns but environmental and social value creation.

Case Study: Unilever's Sustainable Living Plan

Unilever pioneered impact-driven governance with its **Sustainable Living Plan (2010–2020)**. The plan set ambitious targets: improving health and well-being for 1 billion people, halving environmental footprint, and enhancing livelihoods for millions.

Unlike traditional CSR, the plan was embedded into corporate strategy. The board oversaw progress, tied executive incentives to sustainability, and reported transparently on successes and failures.

Results were mixed: some targets were achieved (e.g., reducing waste, improving hygiene outcomes), while others fell short. But the governance model was transformative. Unilever proved that boards could govern for measurable impact, not just compliance.

This case highlights the challenge and the promise: impact governance is difficult, but it builds trust, resilience, and long-term advantage.

The Board's Role in Impact Governance

Boards seeking to lead in this new era must:

1. **Define Impact Purpose** Clarify the company's intended impact: what societal and environmental outcomes align with its strategy and values.
2. **Measure What Matters** Move beyond ESG checklists to impact-weighted accounts — tracking how products, operations, and investments affect society and the planet.
3. **Integrate Impact into Strategy** Ensure that decisions on capital allocation, innovation, and partnerships align with impact goals.
4. **Accountability** Link executive pay and performance evaluation to verified impact outcomes, not just ESG disclosures.
5. **Transparency** Report impact honestly, including failures and trade-offs. Stakeholders trust progress more when companies admit challenges.

Standards and References

- **Impact-Weighted Accounts Initiative (Harvard Business School):** Developing methods to include social and environmental costs in financial statements.
- **ISSB & Integrated Reporting Frameworks:** Moving toward holistic disclosure across financial and non-financial capitals.
- **B Corp Certification:** Independent verification of purpose-driven impact, aligning governance with broader societal goals.
- **UN Sustainable Development Goals (SDGs):** Provide a shared framework for measuring global impact.

Boards that align with these initiatives will be at the forefront of governance innovation.

Impact as Performance, Not Charity

Impact governance is not philanthropy. It is not about giving away profits but about **how profits are made**. Companies that reduce waste, build circular economies, or improve community well-being are not donating — they are creating shared value that strengthens competitiveness.

Boards must embrace this shift: performance is no longer just financial. True performance is the ability to create impact that sustains both the company and society.

Takeaways & Reflections

Impact governance represents the next chapter in the evolution of corporate responsibility. Boards that adopt it will be seen not only as stewards of capital but as stewards of society.

Reflect on these questions:

Reflection 1: Purpose and Impact

Has our board clearly defined the impact we want to create for society and the environment?

Reflection 2: Measuring Outcomes

Do we measure real-world outcomes, or do we focus mainly on ESG disclosures that may not reflect true impact?

Reflection 3: Accountability

Is leadership held accountable for delivering impact — through incentives, reporting, and board oversight?

_____

_____

Closing Thought

The future of governance is not just ESG, but impact. Boards that move beyond reporting toward real-world outcomes will not only satisfy regulators and investors but will earn the enduring trust of society. In the end, impact governance is not about looking good in reports — it is about doing good in reality, and proving it.

Part V Summary – Stakeholders, Sustainability & ESG

Corporate governance today cannot be confined to shareholders alone. The legitimacy of business depends on how boards address the needs of stakeholders, respond to societal pressures, and create value that endures beyond quarterly results. Part V showed how high-impact governance extends responsibility outward — to employees, consumers, communities, and the planet.

We began with **stakeholders and corporate purpose**. The shift from shareholder primacy to stakeholder governance is underway, but fragile. The U.S. Business Roundtable's 2019 pledge highlighted the rhetoric, while Danone's experiment with embedding purpose into its bylaws showed both the promise and the backlash. The lesson: stakeholder governance is not words, but courage backed by systems.

We then explored **ESG as a governance imperative**. ExxonMobil's shareholder revolt, backed by BlackRock and Engine No. 1, proved that investors expect boards to integrate ESG into strategy and accountability. ESG is no longer philanthropy; it is the condition for legitimacy and capital access.

Next, we focused on **climate and environment**. The Shell litigation in Dutch courts showed how climate obligations are now legally enforceable. Climate is not a side issue — it is existential. Boards that fail to govern for climate resilience will not survive in a net-zero economy.

In **social responsibility and the consumer voice**, we saw how boycotts during the Gaza war materially impacted Starbucks' sales and reputation.

Consumers now act as governance actors, holding companies accountable in real time. Yet we also saw that companies with B Corp certification demonstrate how proactive responsibility strengthens trust and drives growth.

Finally, we examined **impact governance**. ESG reporting is necessary but insufficient; the next frontier is measuring real outcomes. Unilever's Sustainable Living Plan showed both the difficulty and the promise of impact-driven governance. Boards that govern for impact — not just disclosure — will lead the future.

Reflection Pause

- Has our board moved beyond shareholder primacy to define a true stakeholder purpose?
- Do we treat ESG as reporting, or as governance integrated into strategy, risk, and incentives?
- How seriously do we govern for climate and environmental resilience?
- How prepared are we to engage with consumer activism — to respond not only to regulation but to legitimacy?
- Are we ready to evolve from ESG compliance to impact governance, proving our real-world contributions?

Part V leaves us with this truth: governance is not only inward-looking, but outward-facing. Boards that ignore stakeholders, society, and the planet will lose legitimacy, capital, and trust. Boards that embrace them will not only survive — they will shape the future of business.

PART VI
TECHNOLOGY, INNOVATION & DIGITAL GOVERNANCE

CHAPTER 21
Digital Transformation and the Boardroom

"Digital transformation is not an IT project. It is a governance mandate that defines whether companies survive disruption or fade into irrelevance."

— ALI KASA

Why Digital Transformation Is a Governance Issue

For decades, boards treated technology as a back-office matter — important for efficiency, but not central to governance. That era is over. Today, technology defines strategy, competitiveness, and resilience. Whether in banking, retail, energy, or healthcare, companies are now digital businesses first and sector businesses second.

Digital transformation is not about automating processes; it is about reimagining business models, customer engagement, supply chains, and even corporate purpose through technology. Boards that fail to govern this transformation risk obsolescence.

What Drives Digital Transformation?

Several forces have pushed digital transformation from optional to existential:

- **COVID-19 Pandemic:** When lockdowns began in 2020, companies with robust digital infrastructure (e-commerce platforms, remote working systems, digital payments) thrived, while others scrambled to survive. The pandemic accelerated years of digital adoption into months, making technology a lifeline.

- **Consumer Expectations:** Customers now demand seamless digital experiences — instant payments, personalized services, and on-demand delivery. Companies that cannot deliver lose relevance.
- **Global Competition:** New digital-native companies (e.g., fintechs, platform businesses) disrupt incumbents by offering faster, cheaper, and more innovative solutions.
- **Regulatory Shifts:** Governments now impose digital reporting, cybersecurity obligations, and data protection standards, forcing boards to prioritize digital governance.
- **Investor Pressure:** Investors increasingly view digital maturity as a proxy for resilience and long-term value creation.

These drivers make digital transformation not only a matter of efficiency but of survival.

Case Study: DBS Bank vs. Kodak

DBS Bank in Singapore illustrates the power of digital governance. Once viewed as bureaucratic and slow, DBS's board supported a bold digital strategy under CEO Piyush Gupta, investing heavily in mobile platforms, AI, and digital customer engagement. By 2020, DBS was recognized as the "World's Best Digital Bank." When COVID-19 hit, its digital systems enabled resilience and growth, while competitors struggled.

Contrast this with Kodak. Despite inventing the first digital camera in 1975, Kodak's board clung to film-based revenue models. It failed to govern digital disruption, prioritizing short-term profits over transformation. By the time the market shifted, Kodak declared bankruptcy in 2012.

The lesson is stark: boards that govern for digital transformation can redefine industries; boards that resist become cautionary tales.

The Board's Role in Digital Transformation

Boards cannot outsource digital transformation to CIOs or IT departments. High-impact governance requires directors to:

1. **Embed Digital in Strategy:** Digital is not a function; it is a lens through which all strategy must be viewed. Boards should challenge management to show how technology creates competitive advantage.
2. **Oversee Digital Investments:** Transformation requires significant capital. Boards must ensure that investments in AI, cloud, or automation are aligned with purpose and create measurable value.
3. **Ensure Talent and Culture:** Digital transformation fails when culture resists change. Boards must oversee leadership succession, talent pipelines, and cultural readiness for digital innovation.
4. **Monitor Risks:** Digital brings cyber threats, ethical dilemmas in AI, and data privacy concerns. Boards must integrate these risks into enterprise risk management.
5. **Demand Metrics:** Boards should not accept vague digital strategies. They must insist on clear metrics: digital adoption rates, innovation ROI, customer experience indicators, and resilience measures.

Standards and References

Boards can draw on global frameworks for digital governance:

- **OECD Principles on Artificial Intelligence (2019):** emphasize transparency, accountability, and human-centered AI.
- **ISO/IEC 38500 (IT Governance Standard):** guides boards in evaluating, directing, and monitoring the use of IT.

- **World Economic Forum Digital Transformation Principles:** provide a roadmap for responsible digital adoption.
- **NIST Digital Identity and Cyber Standards:** establish secure frameworks for digital transactions.

These standards remind boards that digital oversight must be ethical, transparent, and accountable.

Digital Transformation as Long-Term Governance

Digital is not a project with an end date. It is an ongoing transformation. Boards must recognize that technology cycles are shortening, disruptions are constant, and innovation must be continuous.

High-impact boards build digital resilience by ensuring that their companies are not only adopters but leaders of digital innovation. This requires courage to invest, discipline to govern risks, and vision to see technology as the architecture of future competitiveness.

Takeaways & Reflections

Digital transformation is governance in action. Boards that embrace it secure resilience and competitiveness; those that ignore it risk irrelevance.

Reflect on these questions:

Reflection 1: Digital Strategy

Is digital transformation central to our board's strategic agenda, or is it treated as a side topic managed by IT?

_____

_____

Reflection 2: COVID-19 Lessons

What did the pandemic reveal about our digital strengths and weaknesses? How has the board ensured those lessons are acted upon?

Reflection 3: Talent and Culture

Does our board oversee cultural readiness for digital innovation? Do we have leaders capable of driving transformation?

Reflection 4: Risk Oversight

How do we govern the risks of digital transformation — cybersecurity, data ethics, and disruption — without stifling innovation?

Closing Thought

Digital transformation is not optional, and it is not technical. It is governance. Boards that understand this truth will shape companies that adapt, innovate, and endure. Boards that ignore it will find that no amount of compliance or reporting can save them from irrelevance in a digital world.

CHAPTER 22
Cybersecurity and Digital Resilience

"In the digital age, a company's reputation can be destroyed not by what it does wrong, but by what it fails to protect."

— ALI KASA

Cyber as Existential Risk

For decades, boards treated cybersecurity as a technical issue for IT departments. Today, that mindset is dangerously outdated. Cyberattacks can halt operations, expose sensitive data, disrupt supply chains, and destroy trust in a matter of hours.

Ransomware attacks shut down pipelines. Phishing breaches compromise millions of customer accounts. Nation-state hackers target critical infrastructure. Regulatory fines for data leaks climb into billions. In this environment, cybersecurity is not only about defense — it is about **governance for resilience**.

Case Study: Colonial Pipeline Ransomware Attack (2021)

In May 2021, Colonial Pipeline, the largest fuel pipeline operator in the United States, was hit by a ransomware attack. Hackers penetrated IT systems and forced a shutdown of operations. Within days, fuel shortages spread across the East Coast, panic buying ensued, and the U.S. government declared a state of emergency.

The company eventually paid $4.4 million in ransom, though much was later recovered. The bigger damage was reputational: questions arose about why critical infrastructure lacked stronger cyber defenses, and whether board oversight had been adequate.

The Colonial Pipeline incident revealed a stark truth: cybersecurity is not just about data. It is about business continuity, national security, and corporate legitimacy. Boards that underestimate it risk catastrophic consequences.

The Board's Role in Cybersecurity Governance

High-impact boards treat cybersecurity as a boardroom issue, not a technical afterthought. Their responsibilities include:

1. **Cyber Risk Integration:** Cybersecurity must be integrated into enterprise risk management (ERM). Boards should demand cyber risk appetite statements, stress tests, and resilience plans.
2. **Oversight of Investment:** Boards must ensure adequate investment in cybersecurity — from firewalls and encryption to advanced detection systems. Cybersecurity is not a cost to cut but an asset to protect.
3. **Incident Preparedness:** Boards must oversee cyber crisis playbooks: who responds, how communication flows, how regulators and stakeholders are engaged.
4. **Board Competence:** Boards need digital literacy. Without it, directors cannot challenge management effectively. Some companies now appoint "cyber directors" or establish technology committees.
5. **Third-Party Risk:** Many breaches occur through suppliers. Boards must oversee supply chain security, ensuring vendors meet the same cyber standards.
6. **Culture of Awareness** Cyber resilience depends on people as much as systems. Boards must ensure employee training, phishing simulations, and a culture of vigilance.

Standards and References

Boards can anchor their oversight in established frameworks:

- **NIST Cybersecurity Framework (U.S.):** widely adopted standard for identifying, protecting, detecting, responding to, and recovering from cyber threats.
- **ISO/IEC 27001 (Information Security Management Systems):** international standard for designing and certifying cybersecurity systems.
- **EU NIS2 Directive (2023):** requires boards of critical and large entities in Europe to take direct responsibility for cyber resilience.
- **OECD Principles (2023, V.A):** highlight digital security risk management as essential for governance accountability.

These standards make it clear: cybersecurity is a board accountability, not just an IT responsibility.

Cyber Resilience: Beyond Defense

Defense alone is not enough. High-impact governance emphasizes **cyber resilience**: the ability to continue operations, protect stakeholders, and recover swiftly after an attack.

This means building redundancy, preparing for downtime, and ensuring business continuity systems are tested regularly. Just as boards oversee financial resilience, they must now govern digital resilience.

Takeaways & Reflections

Cybersecurity is no longer optional. It is a governance responsibility tied directly to survival and trust. Boards that govern it proactively will safeguard not only data, but reputation and resilience.

CYBERSECURITY AND DIGITAL RESILIENCE

Reflect on these questions:

Reflection 1: Board Competence

Does our board have the digital literacy to govern cybersecurity effectively, or do we rely entirely on management's assurances?

Reflection 2: Incident Preparedness

If a major cyberattack hit tomorrow, would our board know the playbook? How would we communicate with regulators, customers, and investors?

Reflection 3: Investment and Risk Appetite

Do we invest enough in cyber resilience, and have we defined a clear risk appetite for digital threats?

Reflection 4: Supply Chain Risks

How do we monitor cybersecurity across suppliers and partners? Could a third-party vulnerability bring us down?

Closing Thought

Cybersecurity is the frontline of governance in the digital age. Boards that lead in this area protect not only data but the very continuity of the business. High-impact governance means moving from passive oversight to active leadership in cyber resilience. Those that fail will not simply lose information; they may lose everything.

CHAPTER 23
Artificial Intelligence, Data Ethics & Governance

"Artificial intelligence may not replace boards, but boards that fail to govern AI will be replaced by those that do."

— ALI KASA

The AI Revolution and Why It Matters to Boards

Artificial intelligence (AI) is no longer a futuristic concept. It powers recommendation engines on Netflix, fraud detection in banks, predictive maintenance in factories, and generative models that create text, images, and code. The global AI market is projected to exceed $1 trillion in the next decade, transforming nearly every industry.

But with opportunity comes risk. AI can entrench bias, violate privacy, manipulate consumers, and make opaque decisions that boards cannot explain. When misused or poorly governed, AI can lead to scandals that destroy trust. For boards, AI is not a technical issue — it is a governance challenge.

Case Study: Facebook and Cambridge Analytica

In 2018, it was revealed that Cambridge Analytica harvested data from 87 million Facebook users without consent and used it to influence political campaigns. While the scandal was about data misuse, it highlighted a deeper governance failure: Facebook's board had not adequately overseen how data was collected, shared, and monetized.

The fallout was immense: Facebook paid a $5 billion fine to the U.S. Federal Trade Commission, faced global outrage, and saw its brand reputation damaged. The case revealed that data and AI-driven targeting could undermine democracy itself.

The lesson: boards cannot treat AI and data ethics as technical afterthoughts. They must govern them as core strategic and ethical risks.

The Board's Role in AI and Data Governance

High-impact boards must take responsibility for governing AI and data. Their key responsibilities include:

1. **Strategy Alignment:** Ensure AI is used to advance the company's purpose and strategy, not simply to cut costs or exploit data.
2. **Ethical Oversight:** Boards must demand policies on fairness, bias mitigation, and responsible use of AI. Decisions made by algorithms must be explainable and accountable.
3. **Data Governance:** AI depends on data. Boards must oversee how data is collected, stored, shared, and protected, ensuring compliance with GDPR, CCPA, and other regulations.
4. **Risk and Accountability:** Boards must integrate AI risks into enterprise risk management, including reputational, regulatory, and ethical risks. Who is accountable when AI makes a harmful decision?
5. **Stakeholder Trust:** Transparency builds legitimacy. Boards should require disclosures on AI use, impacts, and safeguards, reassuring investors, employees, and consumers.

Standards and References

Several global frameworks provide guidance:

- **OECD AI Principles (2019):** call for AI that is inclusive, transparent, accountable, and human-centered.
- **EU AI Act (expected 2025):** the world's first major regulatory framework classifying AI by risk levels and imposing strict obligations on high-risk systems.
- **UNESCO AI Ethics Recommendation (2021):** adopted by nearly 200 countries, emphasizing human rights and ethical safeguards.
- **ISO/IEC JTC 1 Standards:** provide technical guidance on AI governance, data quality, and risk management.

Boards must align with these principles to ensure responsible AI use and anticipate regulatory requirements.

AI Governance in Practice

Boards can adopt practical steps:

- Establish a **Technology or AI Committee** to oversee digital ethics.
- Mandate **AI audits** to detect bias and test explainability.
- Require **AI impact assessments** before deployment.
- Link executive incentives to responsible data and AI use.
- Engage external experts to challenge management's assumptions.

By embedding these practices, boards ensure that AI is not only innovative but legitimate.

AI as Opportunity and Threat

AI can transform industries — but also destabilize them. For example:

- **Financial services** uses AI for fraud detection but face risks of algorithmic bias in lending.
- **Healthcare** uses AI for diagnostics but must ensure patient data privacy and ethical testing.
- **Retail** uses AI for personalization but risks manipulation of consumer behavior.

Boards must balance opportunity with responsibility. The companies that govern AI wisely will earn trust and competitive edge. Those that don't will face backlash, regulation, and collapse.

Takeaways & Reflections

AI and data governance are no longer optional. They are central to board accountability and legitimacy.

Reflect on these questions:

Reflection 1: Strategy and Purpose

Is our use of AI aligned with our company's purpose, or is it driven only by efficiency and profit motives?

_____

_____

_____

_____

Reflection 2: Ethical Safeguards

Do we have board-level policies to prevent bias, protect privacy, and ensure AI decisions are explainable?

_____

_____

_____

Reflection 3: Data Responsibility

How does our board oversee data governance — from collection to protection — and are we prepared for evolving regulations?

_____

_____

_____

Reflection 4: Accountability

If our AI system caused harm tomorrow, who in our company would be accountable? How would the board respond?

_____

_____

_____

Closing Thought

Artificial intelligence is not only about machines learning. It is about boards learning to govern differently. Those who treat AI as a compliance issue will fall behind. Those who govern it with vision, responsibility, and courage will lead in shaping the future of business and society.

CHAPTER 24
Innovation, Disruption & the Board's Dilemma

"Boards must not only protect companies from disruption — they must ensure companies are the ones driving it."

— ALI KASA

The Innovation–Governance Tension

Innovation is the fuel of competitiveness. Yet innovation is risky, uncertain, and often at odds with the board's instinct for prudence. Boards exist to safeguard stability; innovation thrives on experimentation and failure. This creates a dilemma: how can boards protect shareholder value while encouraging bold bets that may reshape industries?

High-impact governance requires boards to embrace this tension, not resolve it. The goal is not to eliminate risk but to manage it, ensuring that innovation is purposeful, aligned with strategy, and supported by systems that allow experimentation without recklessness.

Case Study: Netflix vs. Blockbuster

In 2000, Netflix offered to sell itself to Blockbuster for $50 million. Blockbuster's board dismissed the offer, confident that its video rental model was secure. Netflix, however, innovated relentlessly — first with DVD-by-mail, then streaming, then original content. By 2010, Blockbuster declared bankruptcy. Today, Netflix is worth over $200 billion.

The contrast illustrates the board's dilemma: Blockbuster protected its existing model, but failed to govern for disruption. Netflix's board, in contrast, embraced risk and redefined the industry.

The lesson: boards that cling to past success die with it. Boards that govern for innovation create the future.

The Board's Role in Governing Innovation

High-impact boards balance risk with opportunity by:

1. **Embedding Innovation into Strategy:** Innovation must be part of the board's strategic agenda. Boards should challenge management: *how are we preparing for disruption, and how are we leading it?*
2. **Portfolio Governance:** Not every bet will succeed. Boards should oversee innovation portfolios — balancing incremental improvements, adjacent growth, and transformative bets.
3. **Stage-Gate Oversight:** Boards can use structured "stage-gate" models, approving funding and support at key milestones while limiting exposure if projects fail.
4. **Encouraging a Culture of Experimentation:** Boards must ensure that culture supports experimentation, tolerates intelligent failure, and rewards learning. Innovation dies in cultures that punish every setback.
5. **Monitoring Disruption Threats:** Boards must stay alert to external disruption — new entrants, technologies, or shifts in consumer behavior — and oversee readiness to adapt.
6. **Talent and Diversity:** Innovation thrives with diverse teams. Boards should ensure that management builds teams with varied perspectives and skills.

Standards and References

While innovation is less codified than compliance or risk, boards can draw from frameworks that guide governance:

- **OECD Principles (2023, I.A):** emphasize long-term value creation, which requires innovation oversight.
- **ISO 56002 (Innovation Management Systems):** provides guidance for structured innovation processes.
- **World Economic Forum's Innovation Governance Toolkit:** helps boards oversee innovation strategy and risk.
- **Stage-Gate Model (Cooper, 1990s):** a best-practice framework for governing innovation pipelines.

These frameworks remind boards that innovation is not chaos — it can be governed with discipline.

Innovation as Resilience

Innovation is not just about growth — it is about resilience. Companies that innovate are better able to pivot during crises. COVID-19 proved this: companies that innovated digitally, adapted supply chains, or created new business models survived and thrived.

Boards must see innovation not as an optional edge but as a resilience strategy.

Takeaways & Reflections

Boards face a dilemma: play safe and risk irrelevance, or embrace innovation and manage its risks. High-impact governance means choosing the latter.

Reflect on these questions:

Reflection 1: Innovation Strategy

Is innovation embedded in our strategy at board level, or is it left to middle management initiatives?

_____
_____
_____

Reflection 2: Risk Appetite

Have we defined a risk appetite for innovation, balancing safety with experimentation?

_____
_____
_____

Reflection 3: Monitoring Disruption

How does our board stay alert to industry disruptions, and how do we prepare to respond?

_____
_____
_____

Reflection 4: Portfolio Governance

Do we manage innovation as a portfolio — spreading bets across incremental, adjacent, and transformative opportunities?

_____

_____

_____

_____

Closing Thought

The greatest risk for boards is not that innovation fails, but that it never happens. Boards that govern for innovation and disruption ensure their companies remain pioneers. Boards that play safe eventually discover that the safest path was the riskiest of all

Part VI Summary – Technology, Innovation & Digital Governance

Technology is no longer a back-office function; it is the front line of governance. In Part VI, we explored how boards must govern digital transformation, cybersecurity, artificial intelligence, and innovation — not as technical details but as strategic imperatives that define survival, legitimacy, and competitiveness.

We began with **digital transformation**. COVID-19 proved that companies with strong digital infrastructures thrived, while those without struggled to survive. DBS Bank demonstrated how boards can lead digital reinvention, while Kodak's collapse showed the cost of resisting disruption. Digital transformation is not an IT project but a governance mandate.

We then turned to **cybersecurity and digital resilience**. The Colonial Pipeline ransomware attack revealed that cyber risks are existential, threatening not only data but continuity, national security, and reputation. Boards cannot treat cyber as a technical issue — they must govern it with the same rigor as financial and operational risks, guided by NIST, ISO 27001, and NIS2 standards.

Next, we examined **artificial intelligence and data ethics**. The Cambridge Analytica scandal showed how weak oversight of data and algorithms can undermine democracy itself. Boards must govern AI with responsibility — ensuring fairness, transparency, accountability, and compliance with OECD AI Principles, UNESCO frameworks, and the EU AI Act. AI is both opportunity and threat, and governance determines which side prevails.

Finally, we explored **innovation and disruption**. Blockbuster's downfall and Netflix's rise demonstrated the board's dilemma: protect existing value or embrace risk to create the future. Innovation is not chaos — it can be governed through strategy alignment, portfolio oversight, and stage-gate models. Boards that fail to govern innovation discover too late that inaction was the riskiest choice of all.

Reflection Pause

Is digital transformation central to our board's strategic agenda, or left to IT?

Do we govern cybersecurity as an existential risk, with preparedness for crises?

How do we oversee AI and data ethics — and are our policies aligned with global standards?

Do we manage innovation as a portfolio of risks and opportunities, or do we allow disruption to blindside us?

Part VI leaves us with a defining truth: **technology is governance**. Boards that fail to govern digital transformation, cybersecurity, AI, and innovation risk irrelevance. Boards that embrace them with courage and discipline will not only survive disruption but shape it.

PART VII
GLOBALIZATION, GEOPOLITICS & MULTI-JURISDICTIONAL GOVERNANCE

CHAPTER 25
Governing in a Fragmented World

"Boards once governed for growth in a globalized world. Today, they must govern for resilience in a fragmented one."

— Ali Kasa

The End of Simple Globalization

For decades, globalization was the assumed path of business. Companies expanded across borders, supply chains stretched worldwide, and governance was focused on scaling efficiently. Boards oversaw growth, compliance with local regulations, and global integration.

But that world has changed. Trade wars, sanctions, nationalist policies, and rising geopolitical tensions have fragmented the global economy. Instead of a single integrated system, boards now face a patchwork of competing blocs, regulations, and risks.

In this fragmented world, governance is not only about growth — it is about navigating complexity, managing political risk, and protecting legitimacy across jurisdictions.

Case Study: Huawei and U.S. Sanctions

Huawei, once on track to become the world's leading telecom provider, was hit by sweeping U.S. sanctions beginning in 2019. The company was banned from accessing U.S. technology, including critical semiconductor components and Google's Android ecosystem. Other countries followed with restrictions, citing security concerns.

The sanctions crippled Huawei's global smartphone business and forced a costly pivot to new supply chains and domestic markets. The case demonstrated how geopolitical decisions can overturn board strategies overnight.

For boards, the Huawei story is a warning: governance must anticipate geopolitical shocks. Expansion into global markets is not only about customer demand but also about political legitimacy, supply chain resilience, and government relations.

The Board's Role in a Fragmented World

High-impact boards must accept that fragmentation is the new normal. Their responsibilities include:

1. **Scenario Planning for Geopolitics:** Boards should demand regular geopolitical risk assessments, integrating them into strategy and enterprise risk management.
2. **Diversification of Supply Chains:** Boards must ensure reliance on single-country or single-region supply chains is reduced, even at higher costs. Resilience must outweigh efficiency.
3. **Stakeholder Diplomacy:** Boards should encourage management to build relationships with regulators, governments, and local communities to protect legitimacy in each market.
4. **Balancing Growth and Risk:** Boards must weigh expansion opportunities against geopolitical risks, avoiding overexposure to unstable jurisdictions.

5. **Ethical Accountability:** Fragmentation often exposes companies to conflicting values and standards. Boards must decide: do we comply minimally, or do we uphold global values consistently?

Standards and References

Global frameworks still provide direction, even in fragmentation:

- **OECD Principles (2023, I.A):** emphasize long-term value creation, requiring boards to consider risks beyond immediate financial returns.
- **WTO Trade Rules:** provide a baseline for global trade, though often strained by protectionism.
- **UN Guiding Principles on Business and Human Rights:** establish global expectations for ethical conduct, even in conflicting jurisdictions.
- **World Economic Forum Global Risks Reports:** highlight geopolitical fragmentation as a top global risk.

These frameworks remind boards that while the global system is fragmented, shared principles remain vital anchors for governance.

Fragmentation as Risk and Opportunity

Fragmentation creates risk: higher compliance costs, disrupted supply chains, sudden sanctions, reputational challenges. But it also creates opportunities: local markets may welcome companies that adapt, regional supply chains may become more resilient, and companies that align with stakeholder expectations may build trust where others fail.

Boards must govern not just for growth in globalization but for resilience in fragmentation.

Takeaways & Reflections

The age of simple globalization is over. High-impact boards must govern for resilience, legitimacy, and adaptability in a fragmented world.

Reflect on these questions:

Reflection 1: Geopolitical Readiness

Does our board regularly receive and act on geopolitical risk assessments?

Reflection 2: Supply Chain Resilience

How dependent are we on single-country supply chains, and what steps are we taking to diversify?

Reflection 3: Ethical Consistency

When regulations conflict across jurisdictions, do we choose the minimum requirement or uphold our global values consistently?

Reflection 4: Growth vs. Risk

Do we balance ambition for global expansion with a realistic appraisal of political and social risks

Closing Thought

The global economy is no longer seamless. Boards that govern for resilience in a fragmented world will protect legitimacy, sustain competitiveness, and seize new opportunities. Those that cling to the old assumptions of globalization risk being blindsided by politics, disruption, and loss of trust.

CHAPTER 26
Multi-Jurisdictional Governance and Compliance

"In a global company, governance is not defined by one code but by the ability to reconcile many."

— ALI KASA

The Challenge of Multi-Jurisdictional Governance

Global companies operate across multiple regulatory regimes — U.S. securities laws, European Union directives, UK Corporate Governance Code, Asian governance codes, and regional frameworks such as those in the Gulf Cooperation Council (GCC).

Each jurisdiction imposes its own rules on disclosure, board composition, shareholder rights, sustainability reporting, and risk management. For boards, this creates complexity: governance must be both **globally coherent** and **locally compliant**.

The challenge is heightened by fragmentation: instead of converging, many governance regimes are diverging. U.S. regulators push shareholder rights; the EU emphasizes sustainability; Asian codes focus on long-term stewardship; GCC frameworks stress local content and government alignment. Boards must navigate this patchwork without losing integrity.

Case Study: Uber and Global Governance Struggles

Uber's rapid global expansion exposed the challenges of multi-jurisdictional governance. In markets from London to India to Saudi Arabia, Uber clashed with regulators over labor rights, licensing, safety, and data protection.

In London, the regulator revoked Uber's license multiple times over safety concerns, forcing governance reforms in driver verification and passenger protection. In Saudi Arabia, Uber adapted its governance practices to meet local labor rules and government expectations, while in Europe it faced lawsuits over gig worker rights.

Uber's story illustrates the governance dilemma: scaling globally without robust governance frameworks creates regulatory battles, reputational crises, and inconsistent practices. For boards, the lesson is clear: governance must be localized thoughtfully while maintaining global principles.

The Board's Role in Multi-Jurisdictional Governance

High-impact boards must manage governance complexity with discipline and consistency. Their responsibilities include:

1. **Mapping Regulatory Landscapes:** Boards must receive clear overviews of governance obligations across jurisdictions, identifying overlaps, conflicts, and gaps.
2. **Global Principles, Local Adaptation:** Boards should establish a set of non-negotiable global governance principles (e.g., integrity, accountability, transparency) while allowing for local adaptation in structure and processes.
3. **Harmonization Where Possible:** Boards should strive to align disclosures, sustainability reports, and governance practices across markets to reduce complexity and strengthen global credibility.

4. **Compliance Oversight:** Boards must ensure strong compliance functions, with authority and independence to monitor adherence to different codes and regulations.

Learning from Diversity Different codes emphasize different priorities — ESG in Europe, stewardship in Asia, family governance in GCC. Boards that learn from this diversity strengthen global resilience.

Standards and References

Boards can anchor their practices in key global frameworks:

- **OECD Principles (2023):** provide a baseline for good governance across jurisdictions.
- **U.S. Sarbanes-Oxley Act & SEC Regulations:** emphasize disclosure and financial controls.
- **EU Corporate Sustainability Reporting Directive (CSRD):** sets rigorous sustainability reporting standards.
- **UK Corporate Governance Code (2024):** emphasizes purpose, culture, and stakeholder alignment.
- **Singapore Code of Corporate Governance (2018):** stresses long-term stewardship and board independence.
- **Saudi Capital Market Authority (CMA) Governance Regulations:** emphasize accountability, local content, and Sharia compliance.

These frameworks reflect the diversity of governance expectations — and the need for boards to harmonize without diluting principles.

The Balance: Harmonization vs. Localization

Boards face a dilemma:

- **Harmonization:** provides efficiency, consistency, and credibility with global investors.

- **Localization:** ensures compliance, legitimacy, and cultural alignment in each market.

High-impact boards manage this balance by defining a **governance core** (non-negotiable values and standards) while adapting **governance practices** (structures, disclosures, processes) to local requirements.

Takeaways & Reflections

Multi-jurisdictional governance is not about choosing one code — it is about reconciling many. Boards that manage this complexity with clarity and integrity build legitimacy across borders.

Reflect on these questions:

Reflection 1: Global vs. Local Balance

Do we have clear global governance principles, and how do we adapt them to local regulatory and cultural requirements?

Reflection 2: Board Oversight

Does our board receive regular reports on compliance across jurisdictions, with clarity on conflicts and risks?

Reflection 3: Harmonization Strategy

Have we sought to harmonize disclosures and governance practices across markets, or do we manage compliance piecemeal?

_____

_____

_____

Reflection 4: Learning from Diversity

What lessons can we take from the strengths of different governance codes (e.g., EU sustainability, GCC family governance) to improve our own practices?

_____

_____

_____

Closing Thought

In a world of fragmented governance, boards that lead with integrity, harmonize wisely, and adapt locally will thrive. Governance is no longer about mastering one code but about orchestrating many into a symphony of legitimacy, resilience, and trust.

CHAPTER 27
Geopolitics, Sanctions, and Supply Chain Governance

"Supply chains are no longer just about efficiency — they are about ethics, resilience, and survival in a world divided by geopolitics."

— ALI KASA

Why Supply Chain Governance Matters More Than Ever

For decades, companies optimized supply chains for efficiency — lowest costs, just-in-time delivery, global scale. Boards focused on growth and margins.

But geopolitical shocks have exposed the fragility of this model. The Russia-Ukraine war disrupted energy and agriculture. U.S.-China tensions reshaped technology supply chains. Sanctions, tariffs, and export controls forced companies to rethink dependencies. COVID-19 compounded the crisis, showing how fragile extended supply chains can be.

Boards can no longer see supply chains as an operational issue. They are strategic, ethical, and existential. Governance now requires oversight of resilience, compliance, and legitimacy in every link of the chain.

Case Study: Russia-Ukraine War and Global Supply Chains

When Russia invaded Ukraine in 2022, multinational companies faced unprecedented pressure. Sanctions cut off access to Russian banks, technologies, and energy markets. Companies like BP and Shell exited billion-dollar assets in Russia. Automakers halted operations as supply chains for metals and components collapsed. Food companies struggled with disrupted grain exports.

Boards faced immediate dilemmas: comply with sanctions, manage supply disruptions, and respond to public pressure demanding withdrawal from Russia. Some companies acted swiftly, enhancing legitimacy. Others delayed, facing reputational backlash.

The lesson: geopolitical shocks test boards' ability to act decisively, balancing compliance, ethics, and resilience.

The Board's Role in Governing Supply Chains Under Geopolitics

High-impact boards recognize supply chains as governance priorities. Their responsibilities include:

1. **Sanctions Oversight:** Boards must ensure systems are in place to monitor and comply with evolving sanctions regimes (U.S., EU, UK, UN). Violations risk billion-dollar fines and reputational collapse.
2. **Resilience Planning:** Boards should demand diversification of suppliers, nearshoring, and contingency planning. Efficiency cannot outweigh resilience.
3. **Ethical Sourcing:** Boards must oversee supply chain ethics — avoiding forced labor, conflict minerals, and environmental harm — aligning with OECD Guidelines and UN Global Compact.
4. **Transparency:** Boards must ensure supply chain transparency through due diligence, audits, and reporting. Stakeholders demand visibility, not excuses.

5. **Stakeholder Engagement:** Boards must balance expectations of regulators, investors, and consumers, particularly when supply chains intersect with human rights or conflicts.

Standards and References

Boards can guide supply chain governance using established frameworks:

- **UN Global Compact:** principles on human rights, labor, environment, and anti-corruption in supply chains.
- **OECD Guidelines for Multinational Enterprises:** detailed guidance on responsible supply chain conduct.
- **EU Corporate Sustainability Due Diligence Directive (CSDDD):** emerging law requiring companies to assess and mitigate human rights and environmental risks in global supply chains.
- **U.S. OFAC Sanctions Regulations**: enforce strict penalties for sanctions violations.
- **ISO 28000 (Supply Chain Security Management Systems):** provides frameworks for resilience and security in supply chains.

These frameworks equip boards to align governance with both compliance and responsibility.

Supply Chains as Risk and Opportunity

Poorly governed supply chains expose companies to sanctions violations, reputational crises, and operational collapse. But responsible supply chains create opportunity: consumer trust, investor confidence, and competitive resilience.

For example, companies investing in local suppliers, sustainable sourcing, and transparent due diligence gain reputational advantage and secure long-term legitimacy.

Takeaways & Reflections

Supply chains are no longer hidden in the background. They are front and center of governance. Boards that lead here protect legitimacy and resilience.

Reflect on these questions:

Reflection 1: Sanctions Readiness

Do we have board-level oversight of sanctions compliance, and how quickly can we adapt to new restrictions?

Reflection 2: Supply Chain Resilience

How dependent are we on single suppliers or regions, and what diversification strategies are in place?

Reflection 3: Ethical Oversight

Do we have transparency on labor, human rights, and environmental practices across our supply chain?

Reflection 4: Board Decision-Making

When geopolitical crises hit, are we prepared to act swiftly, balancing compliance, ethics, and shareholder value?

Closing Thought

In a fragmented world, supply chains are governance. Boards that oversee sanctions compliance, ethical sourcing, and resilience are not only protecting operations — they are protecting legitimacy. Those that fail risk not just disruption, but destruction

CHAPTER 28
Governing Emerging Markets

"Emerging markets are where growth is highest, but also where governance is tested the most."

— ALI KASA

The Governance Promise and Risk of Emerging Markets

Emerging markets — from Africa to Asia to Latin America — represent the fastest-growing economies in the world. They offer expanding consumer bases, natural resources, youthful populations, and rising middle classes. For global companies, they are engines of future growth.

Yet, emerging markets also pose governance challenges: political instability, corruption risks, weak regulatory frameworks, cultural differences, and inconsistent enforcement of laws. Boards must weigh opportunity against risk, ensuring that expansion creates sustainable value without compromising integrity.

Case Study: MTN Group in Africa

MTN, Africa's largest telecom operator, illustrates the complexities of governance in emerging markets. Operating in over 20 countries, MTN has faced repeated regulatory, political, and compliance challenges:

- In Nigeria (2015), MTN was fined $5.2 billion for failing to disconnect unregistered SIM cards, highlighting the risks of inconsistent regulatory enforcement.

- In Iran (2000s), MTN faced allegations of bribery and political entanglement while securing licenses.
- In South Africa, MTN has navigated shareholder activism around its governance practices in politically sensitive environments.

Despite these challenges, MTN has also succeeded in delivering connectivity to millions, supporting digital inclusion, and driving economic growth. Its story shows both the opportunities and the risks boards must govern in emerging markets.

The Board's Role in Governing Emerging Markets

Boards must adopt a proactive, risk-aware, and context-sensitive approach to governance in emerging economies. Responsibilities include:

1. **Political Risk Oversight:** Boards must assess political stability, regulatory reliability, and geopolitical exposure before committing capital.
2. **Anti-Corruption Systems:** Boards must ensure strict compliance with anti-bribery laws (FCPA, UK Bribery Act) and enforce zero tolerance for corrupt practices.
3. **Cultural Sensitivity:** Boards must respect local customs and business norms while upholding core governance values like transparency and accountability.
4. **Local Partnerships:** Building alliances with credible local partners can help navigate political, cultural, and regulatory environments — but requires rigorous due diligence.
5. **Balancing Local and Global Standards:** Boards must ensure local operations comply with global governance principles, even when local enforcement is weak.

Standards and References

Several global frameworks guide governance in emerging markets:

- **IFC Corporate Governance Methodology (World Bank):** emphasizes board effectiveness, control environments, and shareholder protection in emerging economies.
- **OECD Principles (2023, II.A):** applicable globally, emphasizing stakeholder rights and sustainable value creation.
- **UN Convention Against Corruption (UNCAC):** provides a global framework for anti-corruption measures.
- **Transparency International Indices:** help boards assess corruption risks across markets.

Boards that use these references anchor themselves in global best practices while adapting to local realities.

Emerging Markets as Opportunity and Risk

Emerging markets are double-edged. Poorly governed entries expose companies to reputational damage, legal penalties, and financial losses. But well-governed strategies unlock immense value: access to new consumers, first-mover advantages, and long-term growth.

For example, consumer goods companies that invested early in India and Southeast Asia are now reaping growth, while those that stayed away face barriers to entry.

The difference is governance: companies that built trust with regulators, upheld integrity, and adapted responsibly have thrived.

Takeaways & Reflections

Boards must govern emerging markets with courage, discipline, and humility. Opportunity is real — but only if integrity is not compromised.

Reflect on these questions:

Reflection 1: Risk Appetite

Has our board clearly defined its risk appetite for political, regulatory, and corruption risks in emerging markets?

Reflection 2: Anti-Corruption Oversight

Do we have effective systems to prevent, detect, and respond to bribery and corruption in high-risk jurisdictions?

Reflection 3: Balancing Standards

How do we balance adapting to local culture with upholding our global governance values?

Reflection 4: Local Partnerships

Do we have rigorous due diligence processes for selecting local partners and advisors?

Closing Thought

Emerging markets test boards' ability to balance ambition with responsibility. Companies that expand with integrity, foresight, and respect for local contexts will not only unlock growth but build legitimacy for decades. Those that chase opportunity without governance will find that emerging markets expose weakness faster than mature ones.

CHAPTER 29
Global Crises and the Role of Governance

"In times of global crisis, governance is tested not by policies on paper but by decisions under pressure."

— ALI KASA

Why Global Crises Redefine Governance

Pandemics, wars, climate shocks, financial collapses — these are not distant risks. They are realities boards have confronted in recent years. Global crises reshape supply chains, capital flows, consumer behavior, and regulatory expectations overnight.

Governance is tested most during these moments. Strong boards provide resilience and legitimacy; weak boards are exposed. High-impact governance means anticipating crises, preparing for them, and leading decisively when they strike.

Case Study: COVID-19 and Global Supply Chain Breakdown

The COVID-19 pandemic disrupted global supply chains on an unprecedented scale. Factories closed in Asia, medical equipment became scarce, and shipping delays rippled across industries. Companies built on just-in-time models found themselves paralyzed.

Boards were forced to make difficult decisions:

- How to protect workers while maintaining operations.
- How to adapt supply chains for resilience instead of efficiency.
- How to manage liquidity under collapsing demand.
- How to meet stakeholder expectations for fairness and responsibility.

Some companies, like Apple, responded by diversifying suppliers and accelerating digital channels. Others faced reputational backlash for neglecting employee safety or abandoning communities.

The lesson: crises do not create governance problems — they reveal them.

The Board's Role in Global Crisis Governance

High-impact boards must lead not only in stable times but in turbulence. Their responsibilities include:

1. **Crisis Preparedness:** Boards must ensure crisis management frameworks are in place — covering pandemics, cyberattacks, climate events, and financial shocks.
2. **Scenario Planning:** Boards should demand scenario analyses that test strategy against crises: war in key markets, regulatory fragmentation, climate migration, or supply chain collapse.
3. **Stakeholder Balance:** During crises, boards must make trade-offs — between shareholders and employees, between continuity and social responsibility. Transparency and fairness are critical.
4. **Resilience Oversight:** Boards must ensure resilience investments — diversified supply chains, liquidity reserves, digital capabilities — are not sacrificed for short-term efficiency.
5. **Learning from Crises:** Boards must ensure that post-crisis reviews lead to systemic reforms, not just temporary fixes.

Standards and References

Global frameworks highlight the governance role in crises:

- **OECD Principles (2023, V.A):** stress the board's duty to oversee risk and resilience.
- **World Health Organization (WHO) Pandemic Frameworks:** emphasize governance preparedness for public health crises.
- **World Economic Forum Global Risks Report:** provides annual guidance on systemic global risks.
- **ISO 22301 (Business Continuity Management Systems):** sets standards for crisis and resilience planning.
- **Basel Committee Principles (for banks):** highlight governance responsibilities for financial resilience under systemic shocks.

Boards must use these frameworks to benchmark their preparedness.

Crises as Risk and Opportunity

Global crises destroy companies that are unprepared — but they also create opportunity for those that are resilient and adaptive.

- Companies that invested early in digital readiness thrived during COVID-19.
- Companies with resilient supply chains gained market share when competitors collapsed.
- Companies that acted responsibly during crises built trust with consumers, investors, and regulators.

Boards must see crises not only as threats but as catalysts for innovation, legitimacy, and long-term advantage.

Takeaways & Reflections

Crises test governance like nothing else. Boards that prepare, lead, and learn are those that endure.

Reflect on these questions:

Reflection 1: Preparedness

Does our board regularly review crisis management and continuity plans for pandemics, wars, and systemic shocks?

Reflection 2: Resilience vs. Efficiency

Have we balanced efficiency with resilience in supply chains, liquidity, and operations?

Reflection 3: Crisis Decision-Making

In a crisis, how do we balance competing stakeholder needs — employees, shareholders, customers, and communities?

Reflection 4: Learning and Reform

After past crises, have we embedded systemic lessons into governance, or have we reverted to "business as usual"?

_____

_____

_____

Closing Thought

Global crises will continue to test boards. The measure of governance is not whether crises occur, but how boards respond. High-impact governance transforms crises from moments of vulnerability into opportunities for resilience, legitimacy, and trust

Part VII Summary – Globalization, Geopolitics & Multi-Jurisdictional Governance

Globalization once promised seamless markets and efficient supply chains. Today, boards operate in a fractured landscape shaped by geopolitics, sanctions, regional codes, and global crises. In Part VII, we explored how governance adapts when certainty dissolves into complexity.

We began with **governing in a fragmented world**. The Huawei sanctions case showed how politics can cripple strategy overnight. Boards must now govern for resilience in fragmented markets, diversifying supply chains and embedding geopolitical risk into strategy.

Next, we looked at **multi-jurisdictional governance and compliance**. Uber's struggles across London, Europe, and the Middle East revealed the perils of expanding without robust governance frameworks. Boards must balance harmonization and localization, establishing global principles while respecting local requirements.

We then turned to **geopolitics, sanctions, and supply chain governance**. The Russia-Ukraine war disrupted global energy, food, and supply chains, forcing companies to confront both sanctions and ethics. Boards must oversee compliance, resilience, and transparency in supply chains — recognizing that efficiency without ethics is a liability.

In **governing emerging markets**, MTN's experience across Africa illustrated both the promise and peril of high-growth economies. Political risk, corruption exposure, and weak regulatory enforcement require boards to enforce anti-bribery systems, practice cultural sensitivity, and uphold integrity even when local standards are weak.

Finally, we examined **global crises and governance**. COVID-19 exposed fragile supply chains and unprepared boards, while adaptive companies used crises as catalysts for innovation and trust-building. The lesson is clear: crises do not create governance problems — they reveal them. Boards must prepare, decide, and learn under pressure.

Reflection Pause

Does our board integrate geopolitical risk and scenario planning into strategy, or do we react only when crises occur?

How well do we balance harmonization of global standards with adaptation to local contexts?

Are our supply chains resilient, ethical, and sanctions-compliant, or do they expose us to hidden risks?

GLOBAL CRISES AND THE ROLE OF GOVERNANCE

In emerging markets, have we upheld global governance values while respecting local realities?

_____

_____

_____

After recent global crises, what governance lessons have we embedded — and what vulnerabilities remain?

_____

_____

_____

Part VII leaves us with a sobering truth: **global governance is no longer about scale but about resilience and legitimacy across borders**. Boards that navigate fragmentation with clarity, consistency, and courage will thrive in uncertainty. Those that cling to the assumptions of seamless globalization will find themselves unprepared, exposed, and left behind.

PART VIII
AUDIT, ASSURANCE & TRUST

CHAPTER 30
The Evolving Role of Audit in Governance

"Audit is not the enemy of management — it is the guardian of trust."

— ALI KASA

Audit: From Policing to Partnering

Traditionally, audit was seen as a policing function — checking compliance, detecting fraud, and reporting errors. External auditors ensured financial statements were accurate, while internal auditors verified internal controls.

But in today's complex environment, audit is no longer about looking backward. Boards and stakeholders demand forward-looking assurance: does the company not only comply, but also manage risk, create value, and operate with integrity?

High-impact governance requires audit to evolve from a narrow compliance check into a strategic partner, providing assurance that financial, operational, cultural, and sustainability systems all support long-term resilience.

External vs. Internal Audit Roles

- **External Audit**: Provides independent assurance to shareholders that financial statements are accurate and fairly presented. Guided by International Standards on Auditing (ISA) and overseen by regulators, external auditors are vital to market trust. Yet their

failures (as seen in scandals) show the need for stronger independence and accountability.
- **Internal Audit**: Reports directly to the board or audit committee, providing assurance on risk management, internal controls, and governance processes. Unlike external auditors, internal auditors look at broader systems, culture, and emerging risks. Their independence from management makes them critical guardians of trust.

Boards must ensure both external and internal audits are robust, independent, and aligned to the organization's purpose.

Case Study: Wirecard and the Collapse of Assurance

Wirecard, a German fintech once hailed as a European champion, collapsed in 2020 after €1.9 billion was found missing from its balance sheet. For years, external auditors signed off on its accounts despite red flags. Internal governance structures failed to act decisively, and whistleblowers were ignored.

The scandal shook investor confidence, leading to regulatory reforms in Germany and renewed global scrutiny of audit standards. Wirecard illustrates what happens when assurance becomes a formality: trust collapses, markets are shaken, and boards are discredited.

The lesson is clear: audit must not be a checkbox exercise. Boards must demand rigor, independence, and courage from auditors.

The Board's Responsibility in Audit Oversight

High-impact boards play an active role in ensuring assurance systems are credible:

1. **Audit Committee Strength:** Boards must ensure audit committees are independent, competent, and empowered to challenge management and auditors.

2. **Auditor Independence:** Boards must oversee auditor appointments, rotations, and fees to safeguard independence.
3. **Scope Beyond Financials** Boards should expand audit scope to cover culture, ethics, sustainability, and technology risks.
4. **Follow-Up and Accountability:** Boards must ensure management acts on audit findings — and hold them accountable when they don't.
5. **Whistleblower Protection:** Boards must ensure systems exist to protect whistleblowers, whose warnings often reveal what audits miss.

Standards and References

- **International Standards on Auditing (ISA)**: guide external auditors in financial assurance.
- **IIA International Professional Practices Framework (IPPF)**: defines internal audit standards globally.
- **OECD Principles (2023, V.A)**: stress the board's role in ensuring audit quality and independence.
- **Sarbanes-Oxley Act (U.S.)**: a milestone law strengthening audit committees and auditor oversight.

These frameworks anchor audit as a cornerstone of governance and accountability.

Takeaways & Reflections

Audit is not only about compliance — it is about trust. Boards must demand independence, courage, and a broader scope of assurance.

Reflect on these questions:

Reflection 1: Audit Committee Oversight

Does our audit committee have the independence, skills, and authority to challenge management and auditors?

Reflection 2: Beyond Financials

Do our audits cover culture, ethics, and sustainability, or are they limited to financial numbers?

Reflection 3: Independence

Are our external and internal auditors truly independent from management influence?

Reflection 4: Lessons from Scandals

Have we studied audit failures (e.g., Wirecard, Enron) to ensure we don't repeat them?

_____

_____

_____

_____

Closing Thought

Audit is the architecture of trust. Boards that see audit only as a formality risk disaster. Boards that embrace audit as a strategic partner ensure credibility, resilience, and legitimacy. High-impact governance begins with high-impact assurance.

CHAPTER 31
Integrated Assurance and the Three Lines Model

"Assurance is strongest when the lines of defense are aligned, not when they compete."

— ALI KASA

Why Integrated Assurance Matters

Boards often receive fragmented reports: risk assessments from management, compliance updates from legal, audit findings from internal auditors, and external auditor opinions. Each line works in isolation, creating duplication, blind spots, and sometimes conflicting conclusions.

In an era of complexity, fragmented assurance undermines governance. Integrated assurance ensures that all oversight functions — risk, compliance, internal audit, and external audit — work together to provide a **coherent, reliable picture of organizational health**.

For boards, integrated assurance means fewer surprises, better decision-making, and stronger accountability.

The Three Lines Model

The Institute of Internal Auditors (IIA) developed the "Three Lines of Defense" model, updated in 2020 to the **Three Lines Model**, which is widely adopted as a governance best practice.

- **First Line (Management)**: Owns and manages risks, implementing controls within day-to-day operations.
- **Second Line (Risk & Compliance Functions)**: Provides oversight, expertise, and support to ensure risks are properly managed.
- **Third Line (Internal Audit)**: Provides independent assurance to the board on the effectiveness of governance, risk management, and controls.

The model clarifies roles, reduces duplication, and ensures accountability. Boards, through audit committees, oversee how the three lines function and interact.

Case Study: DBS Bank's Integrated Assurance Framework

DBS Bank in Singapore provides a best-practice example of integrated assurance. Facing complex regulatory requirements across Asia, DBS restructured its governance to align the three lines:

- Management (first line) was trained to own risk, embedding controls into business processes.
- Risk and compliance (second line) were strengthened with clear authority to challenge management.
- Internal audit (third line) was positioned directly under the board audit committee, ensuring independence.

Regular "assurance maps" consolidated reports from all lines, highlighting overlaps, gaps, and emerging risks. This reduced duplication, increased efficiency, and gave the board a holistic view. DBS has since been recognized globally for governance excellence.

The Board's Role in Integrated Assurance

High-impact boards ensure assurance is coherent, not fragmented. Key responsibilities include:

1. **Clarity of Roles:** Boards must ensure that management, risk, compliance, and audit each understand their roles and do not duplicate or undermine one another.
2. **Assurance Mapping:** Boards should require consolidated "assurance maps" showing how different lines cover risks, where gaps exist, and how findings are escalated.
3. **Audit Committee Oversight:** Audit committees must oversee coordination between the three lines, ensuring independence of internal audit and alignment across functions.
4. **Holistic Reporting** Boards must receive integrated reports, not piecemeal updates, to see the full picture of risk and assurance.
5. **Culture of Collaboration:** Boards should encourage collaboration between assurance functions, reinforcing trust and alignment instead of rivalry.

Standards and References

- **IIA Three Lines Model (2020):** cornerstone guidance on assurance roles and responsibilities.
- **ISO 31000 (Risk Management Standard):** integrates risk management into governance frameworks.
- **COSO Internal Control Framework:** ensures controls are embedded across lines.
- **OECD Principles (2023, V.A):** highlight board oversight of assurance and risk.

Together, these frameworks provide a global foundation for integrated assurance.

Integrated Assurance as Trust Architecture

When assurance is fragmented, boards may miss systemic risks (as seen in Wirecard or Enron). When assurance is integrated, boards gain a **single, coherent version of truth**, strengthening decision-making and stakeholder trust.

Integrated assurance is not bureaucracy — it is governance in action, ensuring that every risk is managed, every gap is closed, and every voice is heard.

Takeaways & Reflections

Integrated assurance transforms governance from fragmented oversight into holistic trust.

Reflect on these questions:

Reflection 1: Role Clarity

Do our management, risk, compliance, and audit functions clearly understand their roles under the Three Lines Model?

Reflection 2: Assurance Mapping

Does our board receive integrated assurance maps showing overlaps and gaps in risk coverage?

Reflection 3: Audit Committee Oversight

How well does our audit committee oversee coordination among the three lines — and is internal audit truly independent?

Reflection 4: Collaboration vs. Silos

Do our assurance functions collaborate and share insights, or do they operate in silos with duplication and rivalry?

Closing Thought

Assurance is not about volume of reports but coherence of oversight. Boards that embed integrated assurance ensure trust, resilience, and foresight. Boards that fail will be blindsided by risks that everyone saw — but no one connected.

CHAPTER 32
The Future of Assurance

"In the next decade, the most valuable assurance will not be about profit, but about purpose."

— ALI KASA

Assurance at a Crossroads

Audit and assurance are under pressure. Stakeholders demand more than financial accuracy; they want assurance that companies are ethical, sustainable, resilient, and socially responsible. Regulators are expanding requirements, investors are asking sharper questions, and consumers expect transparency.

Traditional financial audits remain vital, but they are no longer sufficient. The future of assurance lies in broadening its scope, deepening its impact, and leveraging technology to provide continuous, credible oversight.

Beyond Financial Assurance: Non-Financial Reporting

Boards now face demands for assurance over non-financial information:

- **Sustainability:** Investors want independent verification of emissions, energy use, and climate commitments.
- **Social Impact:** Stakeholders ask for assurance of human rights, labor practices, and community contributions.
- **Culture and Ethics:** Regulators and boards increasingly seek assurance that company culture promotes integrity, not misconduct.

- **Data and AI:** As AI and digital platforms grow, boards will need assurance over algorithmic fairness, privacy, and responsible use.

This shift means auditors must expand beyond numbers to judge trust itself.

Case Study: Assurance of Sustainability Reports (Big 4 Audit Firms)

As sustainability reporting frameworks (like the EU's **CSRD** and ISSB standards) gain traction, assurance has become mandatory. The Big Four audit firms now offer limited and reasonable assurance over ESG data.

For example, companies in Europe preparing CSRD reports must obtain external assurance for climate data, emissions, and other sustainability metrics. This has created a new frontier: boards must ensure the same rigor that applies to financial audits also applies to non-financial disclosures.

This evolution shows that assurance is no longer a niche — it is central to credibility in global markets.

The Role of Technology in Assurance

The next era of assurance will be powered by technology:

- **AI-Enabled Audits:** Artificial intelligence can detect anomalies, predict risks, and analyze vast data sets far faster than humans.
- **Continuous Monitoring:** Blockchain and real-time data systems enable continuous assurance, moving beyond annual audits.
- **Data Analytics:** Advanced analytics allow auditors to test entire populations of transactions, not just samples.

Technology transforms assurance from retrospective to predictive — giving boards early warnings instead of post-crisis reports.

Auditors as Guardians of Trust

The role of internal and external auditors is shifting:

- **From Inspectors to Advisors:** Auditors must provide insights that help boards strengthen governance, not just highlight failures.
- **From Compliance to Culture:** Assurance increasingly covers "soft" areas like culture, ethics, and stakeholder trust.
- **From Financials to Impact:** Auditors must be prepared to verify ESG and impact metrics, responding to investor demand for "impact-weighted accounts."

Boards must support this evolution, ensuring auditors remain independent while encouraging them to challenge management courageously.

The Board's Role in Future Assurance

Boards must lead the evolution of assurance by:

1. **Expanding scope:** demanding assurance over sustainability, ethics, culture, and digital risks.
2. **Ensuring independence:** protecting auditors from management influence.
3. **Investing in technology:** supporting AI-enabled and continuous assurance systems.
4. **Linking assurance to strategy:** using audit insights to drive long-term competitiveness.
5. **Engaging stakeholders:** reporting assurance outcomes transparently to build trust.

Standards and References

- **ISSB Standards (2023–):** establish global baselines for sustainability reporting and assurance.

- ▶ **EU Corporate Sustainability Reporting Directive (CSRD):** requires assurance of ESG data.
- ▶ **IAASB (International Auditing & Assurance Standards Board):** developing sustainability assurance standards.
- ▶ **IIA IPPF:** updating guidance for internal auditors in emerging areas.
- ▶ **OECD Principles (2023):** emphasize assurance as a board accountability.

These frameworks show that assurance is expanding from compliance to impact, and boards must prepare for it.

Takeaways & Reflections

The future of assurance is broader, deeper, and faster. Boards must embrace it as a foundation of trust.

Reflect on these questions:

Reflection 1: Scope of Assurance

Does our assurance cover sustainability, ethics, culture, and digital risks, or is it still limited to financials?

Reflection 2: Technology and Continuous Assurance

Are we leveraging AI, analytics, or blockchain to strengthen audit, or do we rely solely on traditional annual reviews?

Reflection 3: Assurance of ESG and Impact

Do we provide credible, independent assurance for ESG and impact data to meet investor and regulatory expectations?

_____

_____

_____

Reflection 4: Trust and Culture

How does assurance help our board monitor integrity and culture — the "soft" drivers of long-term success?

_____

_____

_____

Closing Thought

Assurance is the bedrock of governance. As expectations evolve, boards must ensure that assurance extends beyond compliance to credibility, culture, and impact. In the future, the question will not be whether numbers add up, but whether society believes the company is worthy of trust

THE FUTURE OF ASSURANCE

Part VIII Summary – Audit, Assurance & Trust

Audit and assurance form the bedrock of governance. Without credible assurance, trust collapses — and without trust, companies cannot sustain legitimacy in markets or society. In Part VIII, we examined how boards must strengthen assurance systems to move beyond compliance toward impact.

We began with **the evolving role of audit**. Once seen as compliance policing, audit must now provide broader, forward-looking assurance. The Wirecard scandal showed what happens when external and internal audits fail their duty: markets collapse, reputations are destroyed, and governance credibility evaporates. Boards must ensure audit independence, broaden its scope beyond financials, and embrace whistleblower protection as part of trust architecture.

We then turned to **integrated assurance and the Three Lines Model**. Assurance is strongest when management, risk, compliance, and audit work together. The DBS Bank case showed how integrated assurance reduces duplication, closes gaps, and provides the board with a single, coherent view of organizational health. Boards that fail to integrate assurance risk being blindsided by fragmented reporting.

Finally, we looked ahead to **the future of assurance**. As stakeholders demand verification of sustainability, ethics, and culture, boards must extend assurance beyond financials. With frameworks like the EU's CSRD and ISSB, ESG assurance is becoming mandatory. Technology — AI, analytics, and blockchain — will enable continuous monitoring, transforming assurance from retrospective to predictive. Auditors will become not just inspectors, but guardians of trust.

Reflection Pause

Do we view audit as a compliance function, or as a strategic partner in governance?

_____
_____
_____

How well does our board integrate risk, compliance, and audit into a coherent assurance framework?

_____
_____
_____

Are we prepared for the future of assurance — from ESG verification to AI-enabled continuous monitoring?

_____
_____
_____

Do we see assurance as about numbers, or about credibility and trust?

_____
_____
_____

Part VIII leaves us with a defining truth: **assurance is the architecture of trust in high-impact governance**. Boards that treat audit and assurance as mere formalities will be discredited by scandal and failure. Boards that embrace them as strategic, integrated, and future-focused will build resilience, legitimacy, and the confidence of stakeholders in a rapidly changing world.

PART IX
THE FUTURE OF CORPORATE GOVERNANCE

CHAPTER 33
The Next Frontier of Governance

"Corporate governance has traveled a long road: from compliance to performance, and now toward impact. The boards of the future will not only safeguard companies but also steward societies."

— ALI KASA

The Evolution of Governance

The story of corporate governance has never been static.

The Compliance Era (1980s–2000s): Born from scandals like Enron, Parmalat, and WorldCom, governance was about compliance with rules, financial transparency, and accountability to shareholders. Codes and laws like Sarbanes-Oxley reshaped corporate oversight.

- **The Performance Era (2000s–2020s):** Governance expanded beyond compliance to driving strategy, risk management, and performance. Boards were expected not just to police but to guide — ensuring long-term growth, resilience, and competitiveness.
- **The Impact Era (2020s onward):** Now, governance faces its greatest challenge. In an age of climate crisis, social unrest, digital disruption, and geopolitical fragmentation, stakeholders demand not only that companies perform but that they create *positive impact*. Governance is no longer just about profit — it is about legitimacy.

The next frontier is clear: **High-Impact Governance**.

Defining High-Impact Governance

High-Impact Governance is governance that creates value for shareholders *and* stakeholders, builds resilience against systemic shocks, and sustains legitimacy across societies. It rests on three pillars:

1. **Trust** — earned through integrity, transparency, and credible assurance.
2. **Resilience** — built by integrating strategy, risk, technology, and culture.
3. **Impact** — measured not only in financial returns but in environmental and social outcomes.

This is not optional. In the next decade, boards that fail to govern for impact will lose investors, regulators, employees, and consumers.

The Board's Expanding Mandate

Boards must prepare for a broader mandate than ever before:

- **Beyond Compliance:** Ensuring adherence to laws and codes remains foundational, but it is no longer enough.
- **Beyond Performance:** Boards must govern innovation, digital transformation, and resilience, not just quarterly earnings.
- **Toward Impact:** Boards must define and oversee the organization's purpose, ensuring it contributes positively to society and the environment.

This mandate expands the board's accountability — from shareholders to all stakeholders, from today's results to tomorrow's sustainability.

Case Reference: World Economic Forum's Global Governance Community

The World Economic Forum (WEF) has convened global leaders to shape the "future of corporate governance." Its emphasis is clear: boards must become stewards of long-term value creation, embracing ESG, technology, and stakeholder legitimacy as integral to governance.

Though not binding, the WEF's work reflects a broader global consensus: governance must evolve to meet the demands of a fractured, uncertain world. Boards that ignore this shift will be left behind.

Why This Matters Now

The next decade will test governance more than any before:

- Climate shocks will demand resilience and accountability.
- Digital disruption will redefine industries.
- Geopolitical fragmentation will complicate global operations.
- Stakeholder pressure will intensify, from employees to consumers to activists.

Boards cannot hide behind compliance reports or glossy ESG disclosures. They must lead with vision, courage, and legitimacy.

The Board's Role in Shaping the Future

To meet the demands of high-impact governance, boards must:

- **Define Purpose:** Clarify why the company exists beyond profit.
- **Embed Impact:** Ensure strategy integrates financial, environmental, and social goals.
- **Build Resilience:** Prepare for crises, disruptions, and systemic risks.
- **Ensure Assurance:** Verify performance through credible, independent oversight.

- **Champion Trust:** Communicate transparently with stakeholders, even when decisions are difficult.

The next frontier is not about checking boxes. It is about **shaping futures**.

Takeaways & Reflections

Governance has evolved from compliance to performance, and now toward impact. Boards must recognize their expanding mandate and rise to the challenge of stewarding not just companies but societies.

Reflect on these questions:

Reflection 1: Governance Evolution

Where does our board stand — in compliance, performance, or impact governance?

_____
_____
_____
_____

Reflection 2: Defining Purpose

Have we clearly defined and embraced a corporate purpose that goes beyond profit?

_____
_____
_____
_____

Reflection 3: Building Trust

How do we ensure that assurance, transparency, and culture make our governance credible to stakeholders?

Reflection 4: Preparing for the Future

Is our board prepared to govern across technology, sustainability, and geopolitics as part of an integrated mandate?

Closing Thought

The next frontier of governance is not about doing more of the same. It is about transforming the role of boards from guardians of compliance to architects of trust, resilience, and impact. In the years ahead, history will not judge boards by how well they complied, but by how boldly they governed for the future.

CHAPTER 34
Technology-Driven Boards of the Future

"Technology will not replace boards, but boards that fail to embrace technology will be replaced."

— ALI KASA

Technology as a Governance Imperative

Boards have always relied on information to make decisions. In the past, this meant quarterly reports and retrospective audits. Today, technology allows boards to access real-time dashboards, predictive analytics, and digital simulations.

The governance of the future will be **technology-enabled governance** — where decisions are faster, insights deeper, and oversight continuous. Yet technology also carries risks: over-reliance on algorithms, erosion of judgment, and new ethical dilemmas. Boards must embrace technology but never surrender their responsibility.

From Static Reports to Real-Time Dashboards

Traditionally, directors reviewed thick binders of financial reports before quarterly meetings. Tomorrow's boards will review real-time **dashboards** powered by integrated data from across the organization:

- Financial performance in real time.
- Cybersecurity risk alerts.
- AI-driven predictive analytics for supply chains.

- Employee engagement and culture metrics.
- Sustainability and ESG impact data.

Boards that use such tools will be more informed, proactive, and resilient. Those that don't will lag behind, making decisions on outdated information.

The Rise of Predictive Governance

Artificial intelligence enables boards to move from retrospective to predictive governance. Predictive tools can forecast:

- Emerging risks (e.g., cyberattacks, climate disruptions).
- Market trends and competitive threats.
- Cultural and ethical risks based on employee data.
- Stakeholder sentiment from social media analysis.

These tools give boards early warnings, but they also create dependency. Predictive governance cannot replace judgment; it must inform it.

Digital Twins of Organizations

One emerging tool is the **digital twin** — a virtual model of an organization that simulates different scenarios. Imagine a board testing how its company would respond to a geopolitical crisis, cyberattack, or climate disaster — not in theory, but in a digital simulation based on real data.

Digital twins could transform board deliberations from reactive debates to proactive strategy labs.

Risks of Technology in Governance

The future is not without dangers:

- **Over-Reliance on Algorithms:** Boards risk delegating judgment to AI, forgetting that responsibility cannot be outsourced.

- **Data Overload:** More information is not always better; directors may drown in dashboards without clarity.
- **Bias and Ethics:** Algorithms can embed bias, leading to unfair or harmful outcomes.
- **Cyber Risk:** Ironically, the same digital systems that empower boards also expose them to hacking and data theft.

Boards must balance the power of technology with human wisdom, ethics, and accountability.

Case Study: JPMorgan Chase and AI in Risk Management

JPMorgan Chase has been a leader in deploying AI for risk management and compliance. Its systems monitor millions of transactions daily, flagging anomalies for fraud and money laundering. The board receives insights that allow proactive oversight, not just after-the-fact reports.

But the bank has also faced questions about transparency and explainability: can the board fully understand the algorithms driving decisions? The case shows both the promise and peril of technology-driven governance.

The Board's Role in Technology-Driven Governance

Boards of the future must:

1. **Adopt Digital Tools:** Embrace dashboards, predictive analytics, and digital simulations to enhance oversight.
2. **Retain Judgment:** Use technology as a tool, not a crutch — ensuring human accountability for decisions.
3. **Oversee Ethical AI:** Demand transparency, fairness, and explainability in algorithms.
4. **Invest in Cybersecurity:** Protect governance systems themselves from digital threats.

5. **Build Digital Literacy:** Ensure directors have the knowledge to engage meaningfully with technology.

Standards and References

Boards can align with evolving global frameworks:

- **OECD AI Principles (2019):** call for transparency, accountability, and human oversight in AI.
- **EU AI Act (expected 2025):** sets risk-based rules for AI deployment.
- **ISO/IEC 38500 (IT Governance Standard):** guidance for boards on evaluating and directing technology.
- **NIST AI Risk Management Framework (2023):** provides structure for safe AI adoption.

These frameworks anchor technology in governance principles, ensuring boards use it responsibly.

Takeaways & Reflections

Technology-driven governance is not optional — it is inevitable. The question is whether boards will use it wisely.

Reflect on these questions:

Reflection 1: Digital Literacy

Does our board have the skills to engage with AI, dashboards, and digital tools meaningfully?

Reflection 2: Predictive Oversight

Are we using predictive analytics to anticipate risks, or do we still rely only on retrospective reports?

Reflection 3: Ethical AI

Do we have clear policies ensuring that AI systems used in governance are explainable, transparent, and fair?

Reflection 4: Balance of Technology and Judgment

How do we ensure technology enhances — rather than replaces — human accountability and board judgment?

Closing Thought

Technology will redefine governance — but it will not redefine responsibility. Boards that embrace digital tools while safeguarding ethics and judgment will lead with foresight and trust. Boards that fail will discover that the future does not wait for those who govern on yesterday's information.

CHAPTER 35
Global Convergence or Permanent Fragmentation?

"The future of governance will be shaped by one question: do we converge on shared principles, or fragment into competing systems?"

— ALI KASA

The Dream of Convergence

Since the 1990s, global institutions have worked toward a shared baseline of governance. The **OECD Principles of Corporate Governance**, first issued in 1999 and updated in 2023, have become a global reference, adopted by governments and stock exchanges around the world.

More recently, the creation of the **International Sustainability Standards Board (ISSB)** aimed to unify sustainability reporting, reducing the confusion of competing ESG frameworks. The dream of convergence is simple: one set of standards, universally recognized, giving boards clarity and stakeholders confidence.

The Reality of Fragmentation

Yet reality often looks very different. Governance regimes reflect politics, culture, and values:

- **United States** emphasizes shareholder primacy, disclosure, and enforcement through litigation.

- **European Union** stresses sustainability, stakeholder rights, and regulatory oversight.
- **United Kingdom** focuses on principles-based governance and stewardship codes.
- **China** integrates governance tightly with state objectives and industrial policy.
- **GCC and Asia** balance family ownership, government alignment, and local content requirements.

Instead of converging, governance is fragmenting — with companies facing multiple, sometimes conflicting, standards.

Case Study: ISSB and the Challenge of ESG Reporting

The ISSB (established in 2021) was hailed as the "IFRS of sustainability," intended to create a global baseline for ESG disclosures. Many countries, including the UK, Canada, Japan, and Nigeria, committed to adopting it.

Yet fragmentation remains:

- The **EU** insists on its own Corporate Sustainability Reporting Directive (CSRD), more expansive than ISSB.
- The **U.S. SEC** is developing climate disclosure rules independently.
- China and other markets are creating their own frameworks.

The case of ISSB shows both the aspiration and the challenge: while global baselines are emerging, political realities keep full convergence elusive.

Why Convergence Matters for Boards

Convergence brings:

- **Efficiency**: one set of disclosures reduces compliance costs.
- **Comparability**: investors can benchmark companies across markets.
- **Credibility**: global legitimacy strengthens stakeholder trust.

But fragmentation creates:

- **Complexity:** boards must navigate multiple, conflicting requirements.
- **Costs:** duplication in reporting and assurance.
- **Strategic Risk:** compliance in one jurisdiction may expose risk in another.

Boards must decide whether to follow the minimum local requirements, or to adopt global best practices voluntarily as a strategic advantage.

The Board's Role in Convergence vs. Fragmentation

High-impact boards should:

- **Adopt Global Baselines:** Align with OECD Principles, ISSB, and UN frameworks, even if not legally required.
- **Respect Local Requirements:** Adapt to national codes (e.g., Saudi CMA, Singapore Code) where compliance is mandatory.
- **Lead by Example:** Go beyond compliance by setting governance standards that build global legitimacy.
- **Engage in Dialogue:** Participate in industry and global initiatives shaping future convergence.
- **Anticipate Divergence:** Build systems flexible enough to meet multiple standards simultaneously.

Standards and References

- **OECD Principles of Corporate Governance (2023):** remain the global benchmark.
- **ISSB Standards (2023–):** first global baseline for sustainability reporting.
- **EU CSRD (2024–):** expanding sustainability requirements beyond ISSB.

- **US SEC Climate Disclosure Rules (draft 2023):** separate U.S. approach.
- **UN Sustainable Development Goals (SDGs):** global north star for impact.

Boards must monitor and navigate this evolving landscape, recognizing both the pull of convergence and the push of fragmentation.

Takeaways & Reflections

The tension between convergence and fragmentation will define the next decade of governance. Boards cannot wait for politicians to decide — they must choose their own path.

Reflect on these questions:

Reflection 1: Governance Baseline

Do we voluntarily adopt global governance principles (OECD, ISSB), or do we only comply with local minimums?

_____

_____

_____

Reflection 2: Risk of Fragmentation

How do we manage the risks of conflicting governance requirements across jurisdictions?

_____

_____

_____

Reflection 3: Investor Expectations

Are we transparent and consistent enough to meet global investor expectations, even when reporting standards diverge?

Reflection 4: Strategic Advantage

Can stronger governance standards be a source of differentiation and competitive advantage for us globally?

Closing Thought

The future of governance will be shaped by whether the world converges on shared principles or fragments into competing systems. Boards cannot control this outcome, but they can choose their stance. High-impact boards adopt the highest global standards, not because they must, but because it is the path to resilience, legitimacy, and trust in a divided world.

CHAPTER 36
Governance in 2035 – Scenarios for the Future

"The best boards do not predict the future.
They prepare for it."

— Ali Kasa

Why Scenario Thinking Matters for Boards

The world of 2035 will not look like today. Technology will advance beyond our imagination, climate impacts will intensify, demographics will shift, and geopolitics may fragment further. Boards cannot rely only on linear forecasts.

Instead, they must practice **scenario thinking** — preparing for multiple possible futures, testing their resilience against shocks, and shaping governance frameworks that endure across uncertainty.

This chapter presents four plausible futures for corporate governance in 2035.

Scenario 1: Fragmented Governance

By 2035, geopolitical blocs dominate governance.

- ▶ The U.S., EU, China, and GCC each enforce separate governance systems.
- ▶ Companies must comply with four competing sets of disclosure and sustainability rules.

- Supply chains are regional, not global, due to trade wars and sanctions.
- Boards spend more time on regulatory compliance than on innovation.

Implication for Boards: Governance becomes a test of adaptability. Companies that master multi-jurisdictional governance thrive; others are crushed by compliance costs.

Scenario 2: Converged Governance

Global consensus emerges after years of crises.

- The OECD, UN, and ISSB converge standards into a **Global Governance Compact**.
- Companies follow a single, harmonized set of rules for financial, sustainability, and impact reporting.
- Investor trust strengthens, and capital flows more freely across borders.

Implication for Boards: Governance becomes simpler but more demanding — expectations are higher, but credibility is easier to build globally.

Scenario 3: Tech-Defined Governance

Technology reshapes governance itself.

- Boards use **AI-powered dashboards** for real-time oversight.
- Digital twins simulate crises before they happen.
- Blockchain ensures transparent, immutable reporting.
- But over-reliance on algorithms creates risks of "black-box governance."

Implication for Boards: Directors must become digitally fluent. Those who rely blindly on AI lose legitimacy; those who blend tech with judgment lead with foresight.

Scenario 4: Impact-Led Governance

Society redefines corporate legitimacy.

- Stakeholders demand companies measure success in terms of impact, not only profit.
- Impact-weighted accounts replace traditional financial statements.
- Investors prioritize B Corps, social enterprises, and companies with verified impact credentials.
- Boards are judged by their contribution to climate resilience, social equity, and trust.

Implication for Boards: Governance is about stewardship of society, not just the company. The most trusted boards become guardians of the public good.

The Enduring Principles Across All Futures

No matter which scenario unfolds, some truths remain:

1. **Trust** is the currency of governance.
2. **Resilience** is the foundation of survival.
3. **Impact** is the measure of legitimacy.
4. **Accountability** cannot be delegated to technology or regulators.

Boards that govern by these principles will remain credible in 2035 and beyond, regardless of the path the world takes.

Reflection Exercise: Your Board in 2035

Imagine it is the year 2035. Your company has been operating under one of these scenarios. Reflect on the following:

Reflection 1: Scenario Resilience

Which of the four scenarios would our board thrive in — and which would expose our weaknesses?

_____
_____
_____

Reflection 2: Governance Legacy

If stakeholders judged our board in 2035, would they see us as guardians of compliance, of performance, or of impact?

_____
_____
_____

Reflection 3: Preparedness Today

What must we do today to prepare for governance that is more fragmented, converged, tech-driven, or impact-led?

_____
_____
_____

Reflection 4: How Will We Be Remembered?

What legacy will our board leave for the next generation?

_____

_____

_____

Closing Thought

The future of governance is uncertain — but its direction is clear. Boards must stop asking, *"What will the future bring?"* and start asking, *"How do we prepare to govern with integrity, resilience, and courage in any future?"*

In 2035, the companies that endure will not be those with the best forecasts, but those with the strongest governance foundations.

Part IX Summary – The Future of Governance

Corporate governance has never stood still. It has evolved from **compliance**, to **performance**, and now toward **impact**. In Part IX, we looked ahead to 2035 and beyond — exploring what the future may hold, and what boards must do to prepare.

We began with **the next frontier of governance**. High-impact governance is defined not by quarterly results but by trust, resilience, and impact. Boards must embrace their expanding mandate — to serve not only shareholders but societies.

Next, we examined **technology-driven boards of the future**. Real-time dashboards, predictive analytics, and digital twins will transform oversight, while AI will enable predictive governance. Yet technology cannot replace judgment; boards must safeguard accountability, ethics, and human wisdom in a digital-first world.

We then asked: will governance **converge or fragment globally**? The ISSB showed the aspiration for a unified baseline, while the EU, U.S., China, and GCC highlight persistent divergence. Boards must navigate this tension by voluntarily adopting global principles while respecting local realities.

Finally, we looked to **governance in 2035** through four scenarios: fragmented governance, converged governance, tech-defined governance, and impact-led governance. Each scenario revealed both risks and opportunities. The common thread across all futures is clear: trust, resilience, impact, and accountability are the enduring foundations of governance.

Reflection Pause

Are we governing only for today's compliance, or preparing for tomorrow's impact?

How digitally fluent is our board — and how prepared are we to blend technology with human wisdom?

Do we see convergence of standards as an opportunity to lead, or do we cling to minimum local compliance?

What legacy will our board leave in 2035 — survival, or stewardship?

Part IX leaves us with a call to action: **governance is not about predicting the future, but preparing for it.** Boards that govern with courage, foresight, and integrity will not only survive disruption but shape the future of business and society. Those that cling to old paradigms will find themselves remembered not for their compliance, but for their irrelevance.

PART X
THE KASA HIGH-IMPACT GOVERNANCE SYSTEM TOOLKIT

Boards and executives often understand *why* governance matters but struggle with *how* to put it into practice. This part of the book provides ten practical tools — an A-to-Z system — that business owners, boards of directors, and executives can use to **design, implement, and measure high-impact governance**.

The toolkit is designed to be clear, practical, and actionable. Each tool includes a principle, a method, and a way to apply it. Together, they form the **Kasa High-Impact Governance System Toolkit** — a roadmap for turning governance from theory into practice.

TOOL 1

The 11 Keys to High-Impact Governance Mindset

Why it matters:

Governance failures almost always begin with mindset failures. If leaders see governance as a burden or a compliance exercise, the system collapses into box-ticking. Shifting the mindset is the first step toward building governance that creates trust, resilience, and impact.

The 11 Keys to High-Impact Governance Mindset

No.	Key	Explanation
1	Governance is the **Architecture of Trust**	Governance is not paperwork but the system by which an organization builds trust — with investors, regulators, employees, and society. Without trust, no system works.
2	Governance is about **Stakeholder Impact**	High-impact governance considers customers, employees, suppliers, communities, and future generations — not just shareholders.
3	Governance is the **Fusion of Strategy and Risk**	Every growth plan must account for uncertainty, and every risk framework must enable opportunity. Governance makes them inseparable.

THE 11 KEYS TO HIGH-IMPACT GOVERNANCE MINDSET

No.	Key	Explanation
4	Governance is **Culture in Action**	Policies are only as strong as the culture that enforces them. Boards shape culture through tone at the top, consistency, and accountability.
5	Governance is about **Resilience, not Just Performance**	True governance prepares companies to survive crises, adapt to shocks, and recover stronger — not only to deliver quarterly numbers.
6	Governance is the **Board's Ultimate Accountability**	Responsibility cannot be outsourced. Boards are custodians of trust, accountable for oversight, integrity, and stewardship.
7	Governance is a **Dynamic System, not a Static Manual**	Governance evolves with technology, regulation, and stakeholder expectations. High-impact boards continuously review and improve it.
8	Governance is about **Transparency and Assurance**	Decisions must be backed by reliable information and credible assurance — both financial and non-financial. Hidden risks destroy legitimacy.
9	Governance is about **Purpose and Legacy**	High-impact boards ask: *Why do we exist?* Governance aligns the company's purpose with its long-term contribution to society.
10	Governance is about **Moral Courage**	At times, doing the right thing means resisting pressure. High-impact governance requires directors and leaders who act with integrity, even when it costs.

No.	Key	Explanation
11	Governance is about **Future Readiness**	Boards must govern not only for today but for tomorrow — anticipating disruption from technology, climate, geopolitics, and social change.

TOOL 2
The High-Impact Governance Canvas

Why it matters:

Governance can feel overwhelming. Boards and executives often ask: *"What are the pieces I need to have in place to make governance real?"* The High-Impact Governance Canvas provides a **one-page map of the essential elements**. It allows leaders to diagnose what they already have, what is missing, and what needs strengthening. It is both a **design tool** and a **measuring tool** for high-impact governance.

The 6 Dimensions of the High-Impact Governance Canvas

(Each box can be used as a checklist — tick if the element exists and is effective.)

Dimension 1: Leadership & Oversight

☐ Board of Directors (effective, independent, diverse)

☐ Board Committees (Audit, Risk, Remuneration, ESG)

☐ Shareholders / Owners (engaged and aligned with governance principles)

☐ Board & CEO Succession Planning

THE HIGH-IMPACT GOVERNANCE CANVAS

Dimension 2: Systems & Controls

☐ Integrated Internal Controls (COSO, ISO frameworks)

☐ Risk Management (risk appetite, ERM, scenario planning)

☐ Internal Audit (independent, board-facing, value-adding)

☐ Compliance & Legal

☐ Digital Governance (cybersecurity, data, AI oversight)

Dimension 3: Culture & Integrity

☐ Organizational Culture (tone at the top, lived values)

☐ Code of Ethics & Conduct (clear, enforced, embedded)

☐ Whistleblowing & Speak-Up Systems (safe, confidential, trusted)

☐ Incentives & Accountability (align rewards with values and impact)

Dimension 4: Impact & Outcomes

☐ Strategy Execution (aligned with risk appetite and resources)

☐ Performance Systems (Balanced Scorecard, KPIs, ESG metrics)

☐ Stakeholder Engagement (listening, dialogue, responsiveness)

☐ Sustainability & Impact Measurement (SDGs, ISSB, B Corp principles)

Dimension 5: Process Assets & Documentation

☐ Governance Documentation Library (charters, policies, codes)

☐ Risk, Audit & Compliance Registers

☐ Records Management & Accessibility

☐ Knowledge Retention & Learning

Dimension 6: Authority & Accountability

☐ Delegation of Authority (DoA) framework

☐ Segregation of Duties (SoD)

☐ Clear Decision Rights (Board vs. Management)

☐ Accountability Framework (who is answerable for what)

How to Use This Tool

1. Print the canvas and review each dimension with your board or leadership team.
2. Tick the boxes where your governance system is strong.
3. Circle or highlight the gaps — areas where governance is weak or missing.
4. Prioritize improvement actions, starting with the areas most critical for trust and resilience.
5. Revisit annually to track progress and maturity.

TOOL 3
The Strategy–Risk Alignment Matrix

Why it matters:

Too often, strategy and risk are treated as separate conversations — the strategy team dreams big while the risk team lists dangers. High-Impact Governance requires them to be fused: strategy must be pursued within a defined risk appetite, and risk must enable opportunity, not just prevent failure. This alignment is at the heart of resilience and impact.

The Strategy–Risk Alignment Matrix

Strategic Objective	Opportunities	Key Risks	Risk Appetite	Controls / Mitigations	KPIs & Assurance
Grow into new markets	Market share growth	Geopolitical risk, compliance risk	Moderate	Country risk assessment, compliance training, local partnerships	% revenue from new markets, audit reports
Launch new digital platform	Innovation, customer reach	Cybersecurity, data privacy	Low	ISO 27001 compliance, penetration testing, data governance policies	User adoption, zero major breaches

THE STRATEGY–RISK ALIGNMENT MATRIX

Strategic Objective	Opportunities	Key Risks	Risk Appetite	Controls / Mitigations	KPIs & Assurance
Sustainability leadership	Reputation, stakeholder trust	Greenwashing, supply chain risks	Very Low	Supplier audits, ESG assurance, external verification	ISSB/GRI disclosures, stakeholder surveys

(Illustrative — readers can adapt to their own organization.)

How to Use This Tool

1. List your **top 5–7 strategic objectives**.
2. For each, identify opportunities **and** key risks.
3. Define your **risk appetite** (low, moderate, high) for each.
4. Document **controls/mitigations** (policies, processes, technologies).
5. Attach **KPIs and assurance sources** (Balanced Scorecard, internal audit, external verification).
6. Review this matrix annually at board level to ensure strategy and risk remain aligned.

Standards & References

- **COSO ERM Framework (2017)**: Emphasizes integrating risk with strategy and performance.
- **ISO 31000 (2018)**: Provides global risk management principles.
- **OECD Principles (2023)**: Boards must ensure risk oversight is embedded in strategy.

TOOL 4

The Integrated Assurance Map

Why it matters:

One of the biggest governance failures is when boards think risks are "covered" but, in reality, blind spots remain. Risk, compliance, internal audit, and external audit often overlap in some areas and leave gaps in others. The Integrated Assurance Map provides a **one-page view of who provides assurance, where, and at what level of confidence.**

The Integrated Assurance Map

Risk Area / Objective	1st Line (Management)	2nd Line (Risk/Compliance)	3rd Line (Internal Audit)	External / Independent Assurance	Confidence Level
Financial Reporting	CFO, Finance team	Compliance team	Internal Audit	External Audit (Big 4)	High
Cybersecurity	IT Managers	CISO / Risk function	Internal Audit (IT audit)	Penetration testers, ISO 27001 certifiers	Medium
ESG / Sustainability	Sustainability team	ESG Officer	Internal Audit (sustainability review)	ISSB/GRI external assurance	Low/Developing
Health & Safety	Site managers	HSE function	Internal Audit	Regulators, ISO 45001 certifiers	High

(Illustrative — readers adapt to their own context.)

How to Use This Tool

1. List your **key risk areas** (strategic, financial, operational, compliance, ESG, digital).
2. Map who provides assurance at each line of defense:
   - **1st Line**: Management (owns and manages risks).
   - **2nd Line**: Risk, compliance, control functions (monitor and challenge).
   - **3rd Line**: Internal Audit (independent, board-facing).
   - **External**: Regulators, certifiers, external audit, consultants.
3. Assess the **confidence level** (high, medium, low).
4. Identify **overlaps** (duplication) and **gaps** (blind spots).
5. Present the Assurance Map to the Audit & Risk Committee annually.

Standards & References

- **The IIA Three Lines Model (2020)** — clarifies the roles of management, risk/compliance, and internal audit.
- **OECD Principles (2023)** — boards must ensure integrity of reporting and risk management.
- **King IV Code (South Africa)** — advocates integrated assurance for holistic governance.

TOOL 5
The Stakeholder–Impact Heatmap

Why it matters:

High-Impact Governance is not just about shareholders — it is about *all stakeholders*. Boards must identify who their stakeholders are, what they expect, and how their influence could affect the company. The Stakeholder–Impact Heatmap helps boards **visualize stakeholder importance and influence**, ensuring resources are directed where they matter most.

The Stakeholder–Impact Heatmap

Stakeholder Group	Expectations / Interests	Influence (Low/Med/High)	Importance (Low/Med/High)	Engagement Approach
Shareholders	Dividends, growth, transparency	High	High	Regular reporting, AGM, investor briefings
Employees	Fair pay, safe work, career growth	High	High	Surveys, town halls, culture programs
Customers	Quality, affordability, ethical supply	Medium	High	Feedback loops, product transparency
Regulators	Compliance, fair practice	High	Medium	Proactive dialogue, regulatory reporting
Communities	Jobs, environmental	Medium	High	CSR projects, partnerships,

THE STAKEHOLDER-IMPACT HEATMAP

Stakeholder Group	Expectations / Interests	Influence (Low/Med/High)	Importance (Low/Med/High)	Engagement Approach
	care, social investment			dialogue
NGOs / Activists	Human rights, climate responsibility	Medium	Medium	Engagement, sustainability disclosures

(Illustrative — readers adapt to their own stakeholder map.)

How to Use This Tool

1. List your stakeholders (internal and external).
2. Define their **expectations** (what they want/need).
3. Assess their **influence** (how much power they have to affect you).
4. Assess their **importance** (how critical they are to your success/legitimacy).
5. Plot them on a **heatmap** (Influence vs. Importance).
6. Decide your engagement approach (inform, consult, collaborate, empower).

Standards & References

- **OECD Principles (2023)**: Encourage stakeholder rights and engagement.
- **King IV (South Africa)**: Stakeholder inclusivity is a core principle.
- **ISSB & GRI Standards**: Require reporting on stakeholder impact.
- **Harvard's "Shared Value" framework**: Businesses create value by aligning company success with stakeholder needs.

TOOL 6

The Culture & Integrity Dashboard

Why it matters:

Governance failures are rarely due to missing policies — they almost always stem from culture. Boards can have perfect manuals, but if the culture tolerates misconduct, governance collapses. High-Impact Governance requires boards to monitor **ethical climate, integrity, and cultural health** with the same rigor as financials.

The Culture & Integrity Dashboard

Indicator	What It Shows	Data Source	Board Action
Employee Speak-Up Rate	% of employees using whistleblowing or feedback channels	HR / Compliance	High = trust; Low = fear of retaliation → review speak-up culture
Ethical Breach Cases	Number and severity of misconduct cases reported	Ethics Office, Audit	Identify trends; hold management accountable
Culture Alignment Score	Employee survey results on values alignment	HR / Surveys	If declining, culture is drifting from stated values
Incentive Alignment	% of incentives linked to long-term, ethical performance	HR / Remuneration Committee	Adjust pay structures to avoid toxic short-termism

THE CULTURE & INTEGRITY DASHBOARD

Indicator	What It Shows	Data Source	Board Action
External Trust Index	Reputation, ESG ratings, social media sentiment	External agencies, analytics	Track legitimacy in society
Leadership Example	Board/CEO visible actions on ethics (yes/no evidence)	Board minutes, public actions	Reinforce "tone at the top"

How to Use This Tool

1. Select **5–6 indicators** relevant to your organization.
2. Track them **quarterly** — just like financial KPIs.
3. Benchmark against peers or global standards (e.g., Edelman Trust Barometer, ESG indices).
4. Present the dashboard to the **Board/Committee** and discuss trends, not just numbers.
5. Take corrective action (training, policy review, leadership messaging).

Standards & References

- **OECD Principles (2023)**: Boards must set the ethical framework.
- **King IV (South Africa)**: Culture, ethics, and values are central to governance.
- **IIA Guidance**: Internal Audit can provide assurance on ethics & culture.
- **Edelman Trust Barometer**: Annual global trust data, useful benchmarking.

TOOL 7
The Performance & Impact Scorecard

Why it matters:

Traditional performance measurement focuses on short-term profit. High-Impact Governance requires boards to monitor the **long-term health of the organization** — financial, strategic, cultural, environmental, and social. This tool adapts the Balanced Scorecard into a **governance lens**, aligning performance with trust, resilience, and stakeholder impact.

The Performance & Impact Scorecard

Dimension	Key Measures	Example Indicators	Board Oversight Focus
Financial Sustainability	Profitability, liquidity, capital efficiency	ROA, ROE, cash reserves, cost of capital	Are we financially resilient and sustainable?
Customer & Stakeholder Value	Customer trust, stakeholder satisfaction	NPS, customer complaints, stakeholder surveys	Are we delivering value to customers and society?
Internal Processes & Controls	Efficiency, reliability, compliance	Process cycle times, audit findings, error rates	Are our processes effective and well-controlled?
Learning & Growth (People & Innovation)	Talent, culture, innovation capacity	Employee engagement, turnover, R&D	Are we developing people and future capabilities?

THE PERFORMANCE & IMPACT SCORECARD

Dimension	Key Measures	Example Indicators	Board Oversight Focus
		pipeline	
Stakeholder Impact & Legitimacy	ESG, community trust, reputation	Carbon footprint, B Corp score, Edelman Trust Index	Are we creating positive impact beyond profit?
Digital & Future Readiness	Technology adoption, cybersecurity, disruption response	Cyber maturity, AI adoption, scenario testing	Are we ready for disruption and transformation?

How to Use This Tool

1. Select **2–3 key measures per dimension** (avoid overload).
2. Assign **responsibility**: management collects data, the board reviews trends.
3. Use **traffic light ratings (RAG: Red/Amber/Green)** for simple board reporting.
4. Review quarterly at board level — not just the financials, but the *whole system of performance and impact*.
5. Link results to **board decision-making**: capital allocation, executive evaluation, strategy adjustments.

Standards & References

- **Balanced Scorecard (Kaplan & Norton, 1992)** — expanded here to include impact and governance.
- **OECD Principles (2023)** — boards must ensure long-term value creation.
- **ISSB & GRI Standards** — require integrated reporting of financial and non-financial measures.
- **World Economic Forum (Stakeholder Capitalism Metrics)** — provides global measures for ESG and legitimacy.

TOOL 8
The Board Effectiveness & Maturity Model

Why it matters:

Boards are not static — they evolve. Some are **compliance-focused** (tick-the-box to satisfy regulators). Others are **performance-focused** (driving results). The most advanced are **impact-focused** — shaping culture, stakeholder trust, and legacy. The Board Effectiveness & Maturity Model gives directors a **mirror** to see where they are today and a **pathway** to where they need to be.

The Board Effectiveness & Maturity Model

Level	Board Focus	Characteristics	Examples of Board Behavior
Level 1 – Reactive (Compliance Only)	Box-ticking	Minimal structures, weak independence, governance seen as burden	Approves policies without real review; only meets regulators' minimums
Level 2 – Structured (Foundation Stage)	Rules & roles	Policies, committees, codes exist but are poorly embedded	Board charters written but not practiced; committees lack authority
Level 3 – Performance-Driven	Strategy & oversight	Governance linked to strategy execution and financial results	Regular strategy reviews; risk oversight present but fragmented

THE BOARD EFFECTIVENESS & MATURITY MODEL

Level	Board Focus	Characteristics	Examples of Board Behavior
Level 4 – Integrated (High Performance)	Holistic oversight	Risk, audit, strategy, and culture integrated; board diversity; evaluation processes in place	Board links KPIs to strategy; conducts self-assessment; active succession planning
Level 5 – Impact-Driven (Stewardship)	Trust, resilience & legacy	Governance is proactive, values-driven, and stakeholder-inclusive; board seen as custodian of long-term value	Board leads on ESG, innovation, digital governance, culture; transparent stakeholder engagement; long-term succession and continuity planning

How to Use This Tool

1. Assess your board against the model — honestly identify your current level.
2. Highlight **gaps** between today's level and the next.
3. Define actions to move up (e.g., from compliance → performance, from performance → impact).
4. Use it as a **board development framework** for annual evaluations.
5. Revisit annually to measure progress.

Standards & References

- **OECD Principles (2023):** Boards must ensure effective oversight, integrity, and value creation.
- **UK Corporate Governance Code (2024):** Stresses board evaluation and succession planning.
- **King IV (South Africa):** Promotes outcomes-based, stakeholder-inclusive governance.
- **IFC Board Effectiveness Framework:** Widely used maturity benchmarks for emerging markets.

TOOL 9
The Crisis & Resilience Readiness Checklist

Why it matters:

Crisis exposes whether governance is real or just words on paper. Companies with strong resilience systems recover and grow stronger. Those without them collapse under pressure. Boards must actively oversee business **continuity, crisis management, and resilience planning**. This tool provides a structured checklist to ensure organizations are prepared.

The Crisis & Resilience Readiness Checklist

Dimension	Checklist Items	Board Oversight Questions
Business Continuity Planning (BCP)	☐ Documented and tested BCP in place ☐ Critical processes identified ☐ Backup sites and IT recovery systems	Do we test our BCP annually, and did it work under stress?
Crisis Response Governance	☐ Crisis management team appointed ☐ Clear decision-making hierarchy ☐ Defined communication protocols	Who takes charge in the first 24 hours of a crisis?
Stakeholder Communication	☐ Pre-approved holding statements ☐ Media training for executives ☐ Stakeholder mapping for crisis	How do we ensure fast, transparent communication under stress?
Resilience of Supply Chains	☐ Critical suppliers identified ☐ Alternative suppliers contracted ☐ Geopolitical risks assessed	How dependent are we on single suppliers or countries?
Cybersecurity & Digital Resilience	☐ Incident response plan in place ☐ Penetration testing conducted ☐ Data backup and recovery verified	How fast can we recover from a major cyberattack?
Financial Resilience	☐ Liquidity buffers maintained ☐ Access to credit lines ☐ Stress testing scenarios run	Can we survive 6–12 months of major disruption?

THE CRISIS & RESILIENCE READINESS CHECKLIST

Dimension	Checklist Items	Board Oversight Questions
People & Culture Resilience	☐ Leadership continuity plan ☐ Employee safety protocols ☐ Remote working capability	How do we protect our people in a crisis?

How to Use This Tool

1. Distribute the checklist to management and the board.
2. Tick items that are in place, cross those that are missing.
3. Rate readiness: **Green = strong, Amber = partial, Red = absent**.
4. Hold an **annual board-level crisis simulation** (tabletop exercise or scenario planning).
5. Update plans after every real crisis or near-miss.

Standards & References

- **ISO 22301 (Business Continuity Management)** — global standard for resilience planning.
- **COSO ERM (2017)** — emphasizes resilience in risk management.
- **OECD Principles (2023)** — boards must safeguard resilience and continuity.
- **World Economic Forum Risk Reports** — highlight global risks (climate, cyber, geopolitics).

TOOL 10

The Governance Documentation & Asset Library

Why it matters:

Many organizations treat governance documents as paperwork for auditors. But in reality, they are the **operating system** of governance. A clear, well-structured library makes governance accessible, consistent, and auditable. Without it, boards and executives risk confusion, duplication, and loss of institutional knowledge.

The Governance Documentation & Asset Library

Category	Key Documents	Purpose
Board & Committees	Board Charter, Committee Charters (Audit, Risk, ESG, Remuneration)	Define authority, responsibilities, and structure
Corporate Governance	Corporate Governance Code, Delegation of Authority, Code of Ethics & Conduct	Provide governance framework and accountability
Risk & Assurance	Risk Register, Risk Appetite Statement, Internal Control Framework, Audit Plan	Ensure risk and assurance are systematic and transparent
Policies & Procedures	HR, Finance, Procurement, IT, ESG/Sustainability Policies	Standardize processes and ensure compliance

THE GOVERNANCE DOCUMENTATION & ASSET LIBRARY

Category	Key Documents	Purpose
Legal & Compliance	Shareholder Agreements, Regulatory Filings, Contracts Repository	Ensure legal protection and regulatory alignment
Records & Registers	Conflict of Interest Register, Whistleblowing Log, Related Party Transactions Register	Provide transparency and evidence of integrity
Knowledge & Learning	Induction Packs, Training Records, Governance Guidelines	Enable director onboarding and continuous learning

How to Use This Tool

1. Create a **central repository** (digital platform, SharePoint, or governance portal).
2. Classify documents by category (board, risk, policies, legal, etc.).
3. Assign **ownership** (who maintains each document).
4. Establish a **review cycle** (annually or bi-annually).
5. Ensure **version control** so the board always uses the latest approved document.
6. Use the library as a **board resource hub** (accessible before every meeting).

Standards & References

- **OECD Principles (2023):** Require transparency and clarity in governance.
- **ISO 37000 (Governance of Organizations, 2021):** Emphasizes documentation and accessibility.
- **UK Corporate Governance Code:** Stresses accountability through formalized documentation.
- **IFC Governance Frameworks:** Highlight the importance of policy libraries in emerging markets.

TOOL 11

THE AUTHORITY & CONTROLS MATRIX

Why it matters:

One of the most common governance failures is unclear authority — decisions made without mandate, or power concentrated in one person's hands. Delegation of Authority (DoA) clarifies who has decision rights, while Segregation of Duties (SoD) ensures no single person controls an entire process. Together, they prevent fraud, abuse, and confusion, while empowering leaders to act with clarity.

The Authority & Controls Matrix

Decision Area	Board	CEO	CFO	Executives	Control / SoD
Approve Strategy	☑ Approve	☐ Recommend	☐ Input	☐ Input	N/A
Capital Expenditure > $5m	☑ Approve	☐ Recommend	☐ Input	☐ Input	Dual approval: Board + CEO
Capital Expenditure $1–5m	☐ Oversight	☑ Approve	☐ Input	☐ Recommend	CEO + CFO sign-off
Hiring/Firing Executives	☑ Approve (on CEO recommendation)	☐ Recommend	☐ Input	☐ No Role	HR + CEO
Payments > $500k	☐ Oversight	☐ Approve	☑ Approve	☐ Input	CFO + Internal Audit

Decision Area	Board	CEO	CFO	Executives	Control / SoD
Procurement Contracts	☐ Oversight	☐ Approve (>$5m)	☐ Co-sign	☑ Approve	Procurement + Legal review

(Illustrative — organizations adapt thresholds and roles.)

How to Use This Tool

1. Define **decision areas**: strategy, finance, HR, procurement, risk, legal.
2. Set **thresholds** (e.g., >$5m board approval, <$1m executive approval).
3. Map **who has authority** at each level (Board, CEO, CFO, Executives, Managers).
4. Ensure **SoD controls** (no single person can initiate, approve, and review).
5. Review and update the matrix **annually** or after major organizational changes.

Standards & References

- **OECD Principles (2023):** Boards must ensure accountability and control.
- **COSO Internal Control Framework:** Emphasizes segregation of duties.
- **IFAC Governance Guidelines:** Stress clarity of roles and responsibilities.
- **SOX (Sarbanes-Oxley, US):** Highlights the importance of approval and segregation controls.

TOOL 12

The High-Impact Governance Implementation Roadmap

Why it matters:

Governance often fails not because of poor design, but because of **poor implementation**. Boards approve charters and policies, but they remain in files. High-Impact Governance requires a **step-by-step roadmap** that turns frameworks into practice, with milestones and accountability.

The Governance Implementation Roadmap

Phase	Focus	Key Activities	Outputs
Phase 1: Diagnose (0–2 months)	Understand baseline	Governance maturity assessment, stakeholder mapping, document review	Gap analysis, governance maturity score
Phase 2: Design (2–4 months)	Build the framework	Define board charters, committees, risk appetite, assurance map, authority matrix	Draft governance framework, High-Impact Governance Canvas
Phase 3: Adopt (4–6 months)	Formal approval & adoption	Board approval, CEO alignment, policy approval, communicate governance framework	Approved charters, policies, and toolkit
Phase 4: Embed (6–9 months)	Rollout & integration	Training, awareness, culture programs, integrate governance into daily processes	Embedded governance practices, staff trained

THE HIGH-IMPACT GOVERNANCE IMPLEMENTATION ROADMAP

Phase	Focus	Key Activities	Outputs
Phase 5: Measure (9–12 months)	Monitor effectiveness	Apply dashboards (culture, performance, resilience), board self-assessment	Governance performance reports
Phase 6: Review & Improve (Annual)	Continuous improvement	Independent evaluation, board development, annual review of tools	Updated framework, continuous improvement plan

How to Use This Tool

1. Start with **diagnosis** — use Tool 8 (Maturity Model) and identify gaps.
2. Use Tools 1–11 to **design and adopt** governance elements.
3. Train leadership and staff so governance becomes **part of culture**.
4. Establish dashboards and scorecards for **measurement**.
5. Review annually, updating documents, structures, and processes.
6. Repeat — governance is not a one-time project but a **continuous journey**.

Standards & References

- **ISO 37000 (Governance of Organizations, 2021):** Governance as a continual system, not a project.
- **King IV Code:** Emphasizes application and outcome-based reviews.
- **COSO Internal Control Framework:** Cycle of design, implementation, monitoring, improvement.
- **IFC Governance Roadmaps:** Practical approaches for emerging markets.

PART XI

THE FUTURE OF GOVERNANCE

CONCLUSION

"Governance is not an end; it is a living system — the architecture of trust that must continuously evolve with society."

— ALI KASA

From Compliance to Impact

The story of corporate governance began with **rules and compliance**. For decades, organizations designed governance frameworks to satisfy regulators, auditors, and markets. While these systems created order and accountability, they often became **checklists and paperwork**. Too many boards confused compliance with governance — until crisis revealed the gap.

High-Impact Governance is the next frontier. It is not about ticking boxes but about **creating resilience, delivering stakeholder value, and safeguarding trust**. As this book has shown, the path is clear: governance must move from **compliance → performance → impact**.

The Future Forces Boards Cannot Ignore

As we look forward, governance will be shaped by **forces no board can escape**:

- **Technology & AI:** Artificial intelligence, big data, and digital platforms will demand new oversight — not just for efficiency, but for ethics, privacy, and bias.
- **Climate & Sustainability:** ESG is no longer optional. Climate risk, resource scarcity, and sustainability expectations will dominate board agendas.

- **Geopolitical Shocks:** Wars, sanctions, boycotts, and shifting alliances will test resilience like never before. Global governance must be prepared for uncertainty.
- **Generational Change:** Millennials and Gen Z demand authenticity, transparency, and accountability. Companies that ignore them will lose talent and legitimacy.
- **Stakeholder Activism:** Customers, communities, and NGOs now wield power through boycotts, social media, and investor activism. Silence is no longer safe.

Boards that govern for the future must embrace these forces with courage and foresight.

The Call for Moral Courage

At the heart of High-Impact Governance lies a timeless truth: **structures mean nothing without people who choose to do the right thing.**

Policies, charters, and dashboards are important — but they are only tools. Ultimately, it is the **moral courage of directors, executives, auditors, and professionals** that determines whether governance protects trust or betrays it.

Every boardroom will face moments where the easy path is to stay silent, delay, or hide. But High-Impact Governance demands leaders who step forward — not because it is safe, but because it is right.

A Living Legacy

Governance is not about the past, nor even just about the present. It is about the **future we build and the legacy we leave**. A company with strong governance is not only more profitable — it is more trusted, more resilient, and more valuable to society.

The 12 tools presented in this book are not checklists to complete once. They are **living instruments**, designed to be revisited, refined, and renewed as the world changes. Use them not only to govern organizations, but to govern **with purpose, impact, and humanity**.

The Future of Governance is You

The future of governance will not be defined by regulators or institutions alone. It will be defined by **the choices you make in your boardroom, in your leadership, in your profession**.

If you are a CEO, how you set the tone.

If you are a board member, how you hold power accountable.

If you are an auditor or risk professional, how you speak truth to power.

If you are a business owner, how you build trust with your community.

Governance begins not in manuals, but in **minds, actions, and values**.

Closing Thought

The future of governance will belong to those who embrace both **discipline and courage, compliance and purpose, systems and humanity**.

As you put down this book and return to your boardroom, remember: **Governance is the architecture of trust. Build it wisely, live it bravely, and leave it as your legacy.**

EPILOGUE

When I began writing this book, my vision was not simply to document governance systems or to compile best practices. My vision was to **inspire courage**.

Throughout my own journey as an entrepreneur, strategist, and governance practitioner, I have seen brilliant companies collapse not because they lacked capital, innovation, or talent — but because they lacked **governance rooted in integrity**. I have also seen ordinary companies transform into extraordinary organizations because they chose to govern with courage, discipline, and foresight.

This is why I call governance the **architecture of trust**. It is the invisible structure that holds organizations together when storms arrive, when markets collapse, when scandals erupt, when communities demand answers. Without trust, there is no continuity. With trust, there is resilience and renewal.

But governance is not about documents, charters, or codes. These are tools. Governance is ultimately about **people** — directors, executives, auditors, risk professionals, employees, and stakeholders who choose to do the right thing, even when it is difficult, even when it costs.

The real legacy of governance is not measured in shareholder returns alone. It is measured in:

- The employees who trust their leaders.
- The customers who believe in a company's integrity.

- The communities who see a company as a partner, not an exploiter.
- The future generations who inherit organizations that are stronger, more responsible, and more purposeful.

This book was written for **you** — the brave professionals who sit in boardrooms, lead companies, or advise organizations. I dedicate it to those who are willing to suffer, to resist pressure, to take the hard path, because they believe governance is not a burden but a duty.

As you close this book, I leave you with one question:

What legacy of governance will you leave?

If you embrace High-Impact Governance with courage and conviction, you will not only shape organizations — you will shape societies, economies, and the future itself.

Governance is the architecture of trust. **Build it. Live it. Pass it on.**

GLOSSARY

Accountability

The principle that individuals and boards are responsible for their decisions, actions, and performance, and must answer to stakeholders for them.

Assurance

The process of providing confidence that information is reliable, risks are managed, and controls are effective. Delivered through management, risk/compliance, internal audit, and external verification.

Balanced Scorecard (BSC)

A strategic performance management framework developed by Kaplan & Norton that measures success beyond financial results — including customer, internal process, and learning/growth perspectives.

Board Charter

A formal document that sets out the board's roles, responsibilities, structure, and authority.

Board Committees

Specialized groups (e.g., Audit, Risk, Remuneration, ESG) that support the board in focused areas of governance.

Business Continuity Plan (BCP)

A documented system to ensure critical operations continue during disruption or crisis.

GLOSSARY

Code of Conduct / Code of Ethics

Formal statements outlining expected ethical behavior and standards for directors, employees, and stakeholders.

Compliance

Adherence to laws, regulations, and policies. In governance, compliance is necessary but not sufficient — it is the baseline, not the goal.

Corporate Governance

The system by which organizations are directed, controlled, and held accountable — balancing the interests of shareholders, stakeholders, and society.

COSO ERM

The Enterprise Risk Management framework developed by the Committee of Sponsoring Organizations of the Treadway Commission — widely used for risk and control integration.

Delegation of Authority (DoA)

A framework that defines who has the right to make decisions, approve transactions, and commit resources at different organizational levels.

ESG (Environmental, Social, Governance) A framework for evaluating an organization's sustainability, ethical impact, and governance practices.

Fiduciary Duty

The legal and ethical responsibility of board members and directors to act in the best interest of the company and its stakeholders.

Future Readiness

The ability of an organization to anticipate and prepare for disruptions (technological, environmental, social, or geopolitical) and adapt effectively.

High-Impact Governance

Governance that goes beyond compliance to create resilience, trust, and stakeholder value — embedding culture, integrity, and impact into every decision.

Integrated Assurance

A coordinated approach that aligns assurance providers (management, risk, audit, external) to prevent overlaps and gaps.

Internal Controls

Processes, systems, and policies designed to ensure financial integrity, operational effectiveness, and regulatory compliance.

King IV Code

A leading governance code from South Africa that emphasizes ethical leadership, sustainable value creation, and integrated thinking.

Moral Courage

The willingness to act with integrity and make the right decision, even under pressure or at personal cost.

OECD Principles of Corporate Governance

Internationally recognized standards (latest 2023 edition) that provide benchmarks for effective governance.

Risk Appetite

The level and type of risk an organization is willing to accept in pursuit of its objectives.

Segregation of Duties (SoD)

A control principle ensuring that no single individual has authority over all aspects of a transaction (e.g., initiating, approving, and reviewing).

Stakeholders

Individuals or groups affected by the company's activities — including shareholders, employees, customers, regulators, suppliers, and communities.

Strategy–Risk Alignment

The integration of strategic objectives with risk assessment and risk appetite, ensuring growth is pursued responsibly.

Three Lines Model

The IIA framework clarifying governance roles: 1st line (management), 2nd line (risk/compliance), 3rd line (internal audit).

Transparency

The practice of openly sharing information with stakeholders to build trust, avoid conflicts, and ensure accountability.

ACRONYMS & ABBREVIATIONS

Acronym	Meaning	Acronym	Meaning
AGM	Annual General Meeting	KPI	Key Performance Indicator
AI	Artificial Intelligence	NPS	Net Promoter Score
BCP	Business Continuity Plan	OECD	Organisation for Economic Co-operation and Development
BSC	Balanced Scorecard	RAG	Red/Amber/Green (traffic light status)
CEO	Chief Executive Officer	ROA	Return on Assets
CFO	Chief Financial Officer	ROE	Return on Equity
COO	Chief Operating Officer	SDGs	Sustainable Development Goals
COSO	Committee of Sponsoring Organizations of the Treadway Commission	SoD	Segregation of Duties
CSO	Chief Strategy Officer	SOX	Sarbanes-Oxley Act (US)
DoA	Delegation of Authority	WEF	World Economic Forum
EESG	Environmental, Employee, Social, and Governance	GRI	Global Reporting Initiative
ERM	Enterprise Risk Management	GRC	Governance, Risk, and Compliance

ACRONYMS & ABBREVIATIONS

Acronym	Meaning	Acronym	Meaning
ESG	Environmental, Social, Governance	HSE	Health, Safety, and Environment
IA	Internal Audit / Internal Auditor	IFC	International Finance Corporation
IFAC	International Federation of Accountants	IIA	Institute of Internal Auditors
IPO	Initial Public Offering	ISO	International Organization for Standardization
ISSB	International Sustainability Standards Board	IT	Information Technology

REFERENCES & FURTHER READING

This book was not written in isolation. It is built on the wisdom of scholars, practitioners, and leaders who have shaped the field of governance, leadership, and strategy. I extend my gratitude to the authors and institutions whose ideas have influenced my professional development, and whose works I recommend for every reader who wishes to deepen their practice of High-Impact Governance.

Foundational Governance Standards & Codes

- **OECD (2023).** *G20/OECD Principles of Corporate Governance.* Paris: OECD Publishing.
- **ISO 37000 (2021).** *Governance of Organizations – Guidance.* International Organization for Standardization.
- **COSO (2017).** *Enterprise Risk Management – Integrating with Strategy and Performance.* Committee of Sponsoring Organizations.
- **King IV Report on Corporate Governance (2016).** Institute of Directors in Southern Africa.
- **UK Corporate Governance Code (2024).** Financial Reporting Council.
- **IFC (2015).** *Corporate Governance Frameworks for Emerging Markets.* World Bank Group.

Leadership & Culture

- **Kaplan, R. & Norton, D. (1992).** *The Balanced Scorecard: Translating Strategy into Action.* Harvard Business Review Press.
- **Edmans, A. (2020).** *Grow the Pie: How Great Companies Deliver Both Purpose and Profit.* Cambridge University Press.
- **Schein, E. (2016).** *Organizational Culture and Leadership.* Wiley.

- **Covey, S. (1989).** *The 7 Habits of Highly Effective People.* Simon & Schuster.

Risk, Resilience & Assurance

- **Hopkin, P. (2018).** *Fundamentals of Risk Management.* Kogan Page.
- **Frigo, M. & Anderson, R. (2011).** *Strategic Risk Management: A Foundation for Improving Enterprise Risk Management and Governance.* Journal of Corporate Accounting & Finance.
- **IIA (2020).** *The IIA Three Lines Model.* Institute of Internal Auditors.
- **World Economic Forum.** *Global Risks Report* (annual).

Sustainability, Ethics & Stakeholders

- **Porter, M. & Kramer, M. (2011).** *Creating Shared Value.* Harvard Business Review.
- **Raworth, K. (2017).** *Doughnut Economics: Seven Ways to Think Like a 21st-Century Economist.* Random House.
- **Edelman.** *Trust Barometer* (annual).
- **GRI & ISSB Standards.** For sustainability and impact reporting.

ACKNOWLEDGMENT OF INFLUENCES

I am deeply indebted to the works of these authors and institutions. Their writings, principles, and research have shaped my thinking, and I hope they will continue to inspire the next generation of board members, executives, and governance professionals.

For the Reader

This book is only the beginning of your journey. The references above provide a **gateway to deeper learning** in governance, leadership, risk, culture, and sustainability. Explore them not only to expand your knowledge but to **contribute to the cause of High-Impact Governance** — building organizations that are trusted, resilient, and impactful.

www.ingramcontent.com/pod-product-compliance
Lightning Source LLC
Chambersburg PA
CBHW060048230426
43661CB00004B/700